an inconvenient trout

jack ohman

HEADWATER
BOOKS

STACKPOLE
BOOKS

8 99852 00105 7

Published by
HEADWATER BOOKS   STACKPOLE BOOKS
531 Harding Street   5067 Ritter Road
New Cumberland, PA 17070   Mechanicsburg, PA 17055
www.headwaterbooks.com   www.stackpolebooks.com

Printed in the United States of America

First edition

10 9 8 7 6 5 4 3 2 1

Cover art by Jack Ohman
Cover design by Caroline Stover and Jack Ohman

ISBN: 978-0-9793460-7-1

Library of Congress Control Number: 2008931367

preface

In 1988, when I owned only two fly rods (a Sage 690 and a fifteen-buck Phillipson), I wrote *Fear of Fly Fishing.* It was my most successful book. When I signed the contract, I thought that I knew enough about fly fishing to easily complete a seventy-page manuscript. At about page forty, I ran into trouble, both in writing and in a metaphysical sense. I didn't know enough about fly fishing to continue. I was worried about completing the text on time, but, more importantly, I realized that I really wasn't fly fishing enough. That thought alone was frightening, but I had to finish the book. So I read a bunch of books about fly fishing and completed the text. Still, the problem remained: I wasn't fishing enough, and when I did go, I wasn't terribly competent. Oh, I had some vestigial skills left over from my boyhood snagging of small brown trout on the Kinnikinnick River in Wisconsin, and I had caught the odd fish by accident in various streams and rivers in Oregon. Fundamentally, however, my skill level was quite low.

I kind of tied flies (badly) and had one decent rod and reel but, overall, I had no clue.

For example, I could not:

- Cast upstream to rising trout.
- Successfully execute any sort of long cast, let alone double-haul.
- Tie a dry fly that lived up to its intended function.
- Tell you what a PMD was.
- Crack the Deschutes.

And so on. Cracking the Deschutes became my Holy Grail. I had gone to the Deschutes many times with almost no success whatsoever. The Deschutes is, of course, one of the premier fly-fishing rivers in the United States, and, I suspect, one of the most difficult to fish. It is counterintuitive compared to the majority of rivers in our country. It is fished almost backwards— throw back to the bank, hang off low branches by your pinky, cast behind your back while executing a double

3

axel, and try not to hook yourself in the back of the head with Golden Stones in a fifty-mile-per-hour wind.

I embarked on a crash course to Get A Clue. I had a lot of help, in the form of several cherished friendships over the years. Jim Ramsey, an Oregon rancher and trout *bon vivant,* and Dick Thomas, a brilliant former *Oregonian* editor and reporter, were most responsible for me figuring it all out. Dick was my first fishing buddy in Oregon, along with Steve Carter, another *Oregonian* reporter and great friend. There are others, some living and some long gone now, but these two fishermen were early mentors. Jim Ramsey told me that he was going to give me a graduate course in trout fishing, which he did, in spades. In fact, between these guys, I really got to the point where I didn't feel like breaking my rod and crying like a six-year-old after each trip. If you don't learn something new every time you go out, even at age forty-seven, you're just not trying hard enough. And after about six or eight years of actually thinking about what the hell I was doing, I got to the point where I could reliably expect to catch fish. And if I didn't, well, that was the fault of the Deschutes. Fly fishermen can be arrogant bastards.

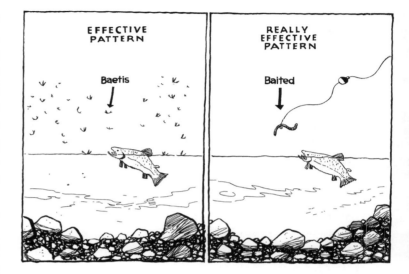

I became one.

Well, maybe not arrogant, but confident enough, I guess. Until I met another guy named Rich McIntyre.

Rich McIntyre is, shall we say, confident. Rich and his wife, Karen, ran a fly-fishing lodge in the Klamath Basin for about ten years, until they decided to get out of the hustle and bustle of rural Oregon and head over to Sun Valley, where, the other day, Rich called me on his cell phone while on the Big Wood after catching an 18-inch rainbow. In the words of Richard Nixon, calling someone on a cell phone while fly fishing is ". . . wrong, that's for sure," but it's the twenty-first century. Rich applies maximum effort to all pursuits, and particularly to fly fishing, where he has rightly referred to himself as the Heinrich Himmler of fly-casting instruction. I learned how to double haul from Rich and how to lake fish from Rich but, sadly, did not learn Rich's real estate acumen. Too busy working on the double haul.

I fish all the time with David Reinhard, a great friend and a fine, if sometimes politically misguided, columnist. We constantly complain about each other's politics, politely, but we can always find common ground (water?) while fishing. There are others I have fished with over the years: Dave Talbot, Eric Talbot, Allan Burdick, Don Burdick, John Ratterman, the immortal Phil Cogswell, Jack Hart, and numerous others who will forgive me for not listing them. Bob Landauer, a kind and brilliant man, hired me to work at *The Oregonian* in 1983, giving me a wonderful gift for life: getting to live here.

Finally, my dad, John Ohman, was the guy who started all this. He was always taking me fishing, even if it wasn't fly fishing. It was a great bonding thing for us even when we suffered through the teen years (I wasn't that bad), and he was the Number One Cheerleader for not only fly fishing, but all the things I really wanted to do in life, including become a cartoonist (once it became clear I had no talent for scientific research). Thank you, Dad, for leaving that fly-fishing stuff around in the garage.

Which brings me to the present. Writing another fly-fishing book over the success of *Fear of Fly Fishing* is a daunting challenge. I know more now than I did then, so I'm going to cover this water again. You never know if there's another fish in the slot you fished before.

—Jack Ohman
Portland, Oregon
March 20, 2008

5

trout menu

Most fly fishermen in the United States have experience with six species of trout: the rainbow, the brown, the brookie, the steelhead, the golden, and the cutthroat. I don't have a personal favorite; all of them are perfectly welcome to jump at my fly pattern, since I have devoted much of my life and career to their pursuit. A woman I know who is fond of sushi has repeatedly expressed amazement at this, particularly the notion of catch and release.

"You mean . . . um . . . you don't eat them?"

"No. Not really. No."

"Why the hell would you do that?"

That's a really good question to which I have no sensible answer. But, anyway, here are thumbnails of the targets of our obsession . . . er . . . hobby . . .

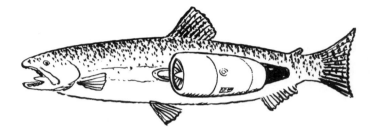

RAINBOW TROUT
Oncorhynchus turbo

Rainbow Trout

Certainly the most discussed species, the rainbow seems to be powered by some sort of bizarre steroid or jet engine that makes it dramatically more energetic (apart from the steelhead) than its colleagues. When you hook a rainbow, there is no question in your mind that you've hooked a rainbow. The rainbow's sheer fighting power, NBA-like manic electric leaps, and its uncanny ability to analyze and reject whatever you put in front of it makes you feel that if a fish could get a Ph.D., the rainbow would have one—in a hard science. The rainbow almost seems like a Fantastic Four hero with some other-worldly superpower to confound the most determined gear-laden pursuer. You can put on your own superhero utility belt, pull out every single object to subdue and vanquish the rainbow, and he will spit in your face, chuckle ominously, and then figure out a way to trip you as you wade back to the bank.

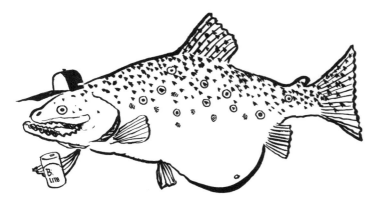

BROWN TROUT
Salmo bubba

Brown Trout

If any trout could be classified as having a personality, the brown's would be Good Ol' Boy. I sometimes visualize the brown trout holed up underneath the cutbank in a Barcalounger, watching NASCAR, eating a buffalo wing (a great pattern in deer hair for a brown), and sipping his seventh cold one of the morning. Brown trout can reach enormous size, have actual bellies (some of which have hair), and seem, once hooked, to wallow rather than fight. A gorgeous species, the brown can at times seem almost comically nonselective, and then turn into some sort of trout restaurant critic, spurning every edible-looking offering. Browns are mostly butter-colored on the lower body, which is actual butter. They love reservoirs, where they can pick off six-inch chubs like a starving Norwegian ripping into a can of kippered herring.

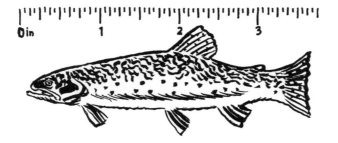

BROOK TROUT
Salvelinus dinki

Brook Trout

The brookie is an endearing little species, beloved by all fly fishermen for its stunning iridescent speckles and olive-green vermiculations on its back (those are the squiggly things on top, and the only time you ever hear the word "vermiculation" in reference to anything). It's technically a char, not a trout, but I leave that to the fishery biologists—who cares? I always think of classic East Coast Cane/Tweed/Briar/Hendrickson/Harvard-Yale Game/Trilateral Commission Member/Prepped With George Bush 41/Started the Vietnam War/J. P. Morgan/Gilded Age/Pampered Trust Fund, baby-type fly fishermen when I think about the brook trout, but that's me. I live in the West, where they dump them in high mountain lakes for backpackers to eat in the event they run out of PowerBars. The brook trout can grow to lengths of over five inches and weigh in at more than .000000000000007 grams, given a rich and plentiful food supply. There used to be almost unlimited numbers of brook trout back East, but a fly-fishing writer named Theodore Gordon had caught, killed, and eaten all of them by 1915.

Cutthroat Trout

Aren't they all? Western anglers have a particular soft spot for this species, which suffers from a somewhat undeserved reputation as a bit forgiving, even lackadaisical, in the fighting department. True, they are not as aggressive as the rainbow, but they look fierce, which is half the battle. The scary redness on the gill plate and the faux dribbles of Hollywood-like blood on the underside of its jaw give the cutt a menacing demeanor

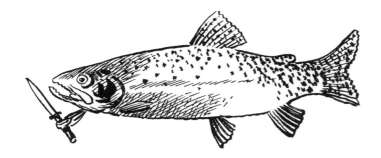

CUTTHROAT TROUT
Oncorhynchus ruthlessi

STEELHEAD TROUT
Oncorhynchus submarina

which masks the sometimes gentle docility of its takes. Sure, I have had cutts float to the surface like a sheet of ruled notebook paper after ninety seconds, but the higher-elevation cutts seem to be very nearly as peppy as the rainbow. Instead of aerial showiness, a good-size cutt will turn to one side like a garbage can lid in current and defy any sort of efforts to bring him in. The cutts also have an impressive row of particularly sharp teeth, which have led my thumb to look like it's been through a three hole punch.

Steelhead Trout

Because this is perhaps the most mysterious of all the trout species, the pursuit of the steelhead has reached almost mythic proportions, due to its starring role in the film *Run Silent, Run Deep,* where it played a submarine. I know many Western fly fishermen who have not only made the steelhead their number-one prey but also have started a weird religious cult around it (Tom Cruise, beware). Fishing for steelhead is most enjoyably performed while standing in a very fast coastal river, naked but for hip boots, while it's 33 degrees, sleeting, hailing, and there are theater nuclear weapons being detonated ten miles away. Steelheaders (a nickname, not a medical condition) are a hardy band of highly skilled fishermen who like nothing better than to make 999,998 false casts before actually catching a steelhead. That's cool. I totally get that. Downside: steelhead flies are often mistaken for badly designed stripper outfits.

Golden Trout

Some sort of mythical beast, like a dragon, unicorn, Sasquatch, or steelhead, the golden is a stunningly radiant yellow-orange, and each time I have caught one, it startles me when I lift it out of the water. The biggest one I ever caught was 14 inches, and that would fall under the category of lunker for a golden. They are, in short, California cool. They know that they're the *sine qua non* (Latin for "without any body weight") of trout, the Holy Grail, the species you can't

GOLDEN TROUT
Oncorhynchus dude

park your 12 MPG SUV next to the river, have three beers, two White Owls, and catch one. No. You have to walk. Uphill. For miles. With 55-pound backpacks. Stop and rest. Take a hit off the oxygen canister. Greet Sherpas. Walk some more. Get out gaiters, ice axes, and crampons. Stop and have a chat with Jon Krakauer over a boiling stove of delicious Mountain House. Step over frozen bodies zipped up in sleeping bags until the spring thaw. Then you can make a cast.

starting to fly fish

Like any drug, rarely does anyone just start doing something expensive and addictive without a proper dollop of peer pressure. Fly fishing is no exception. It's usually some well-intentioned friend who tells you that fly fishing is "fun," and "all the cool people are doing it," and that you "should just try it once."

Okay, maybe I got the dialogue from a drug movie I saw in junior high school in the 1970s, but it's kind of the same thing. I have never really forgiven a few people for giving me a hobby that is way more expensive than bowling or Porsche collecting.

My dad, who now graciously acknowledges me as a better fly fisherman, had a fly rod and some fly-tying stuff in the basement. I remember some dubbing wax, from which I enjoyed making little sculptures, and some weird feathers, and lots of hooks. Dad had this friend Rod (yes, his real name), who lived in a cabin outside Marquette with his dog, and pretty much all he did was hunt and fly fish. I would often hear about how Rod caught this or that, while my dad was putting in long hours repairing my tricycle or cleaning up spilled milkshakes in the backseat instead.

My fishing life then was still very worm-centric and sunfish-based, but that's fine. No one gets hurt except the worm, and even then, I am still not convinced that worms ever die. You can break them into three pieces and they're still squirming around a half hour later. Plus, my dad had this thing called a Bob-Bet Bait Box that had an advertising slogan: Just Half a Turn and There's Your Worm. I wish advertising today was as straightforward. It was a rather ingenious little device you could slip on your belt. Spin it, flip open the lid, and boom! You could put on a worm without having to cut your hand on the edge of the coffee can.

So when we moved to Minnesota after a four-year hiatus back East, I was ready to try fly fishing. I got out Dad's fly rod (a Shakespeare) and his reel (a Pflueger Medalist) and tied on one of his flies (a Red

Ibis). I went down to the lake we lived by, and, over the course of several years using the fly rod caught 236,901,021,445,019,345 crappies. And two bass. Then I met this kid, Lars, who was an actual fly fisherman and tied actual flies. He had this friend, Tim, and they used to go over to the Kinnikinnick River, which is in and around River Falls, Wisconsin.

Another kid, Chuck, who wanted to learn how to fly fish came along as well. There was a fly-tying club at our junior high school, and Lars would show up with his Thompson "A" vise and tie Swisher and Richards no-hackle flies. Chuck and I would tie with our five dollar tying kits assembled in a fourth-world nation (don't ever buy a fly-tying kit—they just confuse the recipient). Unfortunately, Chuck was colorblind, and so he would produce very large flies with chartreuse bodies and purple hackle. Mine were not much better.

After awhile, I developed Gear Envy. This is the fatal moment in any fly fisherman's life.

I had to get a Thompson Model "A" vise.

Now.

I worked a lawn job and got a paper route. I saved and saved. The Thompson "A" was $21, then an astro-

nomical figure. Meanwhile, there were still movies to go to and ninth grade girls to chase, and they cost money. I had a hard time getting to $21.

Then I found out about the Thompson "B."

The Thompson "B," which I suspect they don't make anymore, had the same jaws as the "A," but instead of a lever handle, it had a large red knob that you would turn to increase and decrease the tension. It was eight dollars.

It was gonna be the "B." I think it's the same moment and sensation in your adult life when you theoretically make enough money to buy the BMW, but you have three kids, so you have to get the Dodge minivan.

So I got the "B." I still have it, use it, and it works fine, even if it's a bit on the Soviet side in terms of design concept.

This really didn't move my fly tying forward that much. I struggled for years with it and stopped doing it for a while. I took that hiatus to get more into bass, northern, and walleye fishing. But the fly-fishing impulse was still nagging at me.

In 1983, I moved out to Oregon to take a job at *The Oregonian.* I viewed this as my golden opportunity to get a new lease on life with fly fishing, and I had a number of friendly colleagues who were more than willing to show me the ropes. I still fish with all of them regularly twenty-five years later.

But there was a catch: I had just discovered the Keep Up with the Joneses aspect to fly fishing. That meant a trip to Kaufmann's Streamborn, a well-known fly shop not only in Oregon but nationally. A trip to Kaufmann's meant one had to get serious. Sage. Orvis.

Winston. Scott. My new friends all had them, and in order not to look too much like the prenatal rookie dope, I got the Sage/Orvis outfit. I should have known something was up when this guy Gordon, who sold me the rod, made a forty-foot cast with his hands and no rod. It's still the single most impressive thing I've ever seen.

Then I spent about ten years not going fishing enough. Life intervened with children and mortgages and making sure the garage was clean. When I did go, it was usually a pretty frustrating experience. I mean, I would catch some, usually on nymphs, but dry-fly fishing was still a daunting experience. I had succumbed to Nice Gear/Not up to the Challenge Syndrome. I vowed to get better.

There was an intervention. I needed help. With the assistance and support of several friends, I checked myself into the Betty Ford Center for Fly-Fishing Recovery. Okay, there's no such thing. But it was something like that. I had to unlearn bad habits, like not catching anything and falling spectacularly.

Then two things happened: First, I fished not often, not a lot, but all the time. Every week. In snow. In rain.

In sleet. Drive 220 miles, one way, fish for four or five hours, drive back 220 miles. No one was going to keep me from my appointed rounds. And second, did I catch fish! I caught twelve-pound rainbows. I caught six-pound browns. I caught four-pound brookies. I went on expensive guided trips. I went to private ranches. I fished tiny creeks, lakes, major rivers, drainage ditches, puddles, swamps, toilets . . . whatever body of water was around, or not, I fished it.

I became irritating, even compulsive, on the subject of fly fishing. I bought two-weights, three-weights, four-weights, five-weights, and six-weights. I bought the Wheatley fly box with the little spring windows. I bought two cane rods from the 1930s. I bought books that had hundreds of pages devoted to emergers.

That's just wrong.

I even read the entire diaries of Theodore Gordon. Every single word. In the original Greek. Backwards.

And that's just for starters.

These days, I've settled into a fairly good rhythm of fishing . . . slightly not enough, but still enough to say I go every two or three weeks when the weather's decent. I want to go more.

Oh, yeah. I also think I need another five-weight.

. . . no one has successfully tied an Albright Knot?

. . . the Cuyahoga River caught fire in 1970, and that really screwed up the hatch?

. . . that muskellunge will eat whole ducks, but trout will only eat duck feathers?

odd couples and soul mates: angling partners

If you go fishing enough, you will usually go with someone else. Even though fly fishing is supposed to be a lonely, quasi-religious pursuit, the odds are you will wind up either with a partner or a group. Large-group fly fishing is my last option, not because of the personalities of the individuals, but because you end up having to carve up good water four or six ways. Or more. I have a small number of friends and relations who I go fishing with regularly. I have my preferences, but none of them, of course, correspond to the following types:

Mr. Gear

Mr. Gear and I parted company a few years ago over an incident that involved me using the wrong kind of leader material. All we ever talked about was gear. "You use that stupid Climax leader material? I'm only using fluorocarbon now . . . get with it." "The Hardy Princess is the only reel. Period. Your CFO III sucks."

Mr. Incompetent

If I hear "What pattern are you using?" or "Should I switch to 6X?" one more time from this guy, I'm going to start eating *Baetis.* These are always the guys who tell you with fervent conviction that they are actual fly fishermen. They describe their gear, fish they have theoretically caught, famous rivers they've fished, and then proceed to demonstrate that anything more complex than a ten-foot cast is a rumor.

Mr. Rigid

This guy will only fish a certain way, as in "I have always caught fish on a size 6 Lead Wing Coachmen,

and I will continue to fish this size 6 Lead Wing Coachman even though there is a size 18 Pale Morning Dun spinnerfall." He gets angrier and angrier as you pull in fish after fish, muttering softly about the immutability of his size 6 Lead Wing Coachman.

Mr. Conspiracy

He'll say, "You know damn well the State Department of Natural Resources is secretly manipulating the water levels to accommodate nymph fishing, and that the major tackle manufacturers are engaging in collusion to make us pay $550 for a rod, and that Whirling Disease is closely related to the anthrax outbreak, and that the International Gore-Tex Conspiracy has rendered all of our fishing clothing obsolete, and that Dick Cheney is a well-known fly fisherman who wants to make everyone pay to go fishing."

Mr. Snob

"My God, man," he'll assert after a few glasses of chardonnay, "you don't really still fish with a two-piece rod, do you? I mean, for the love of God, get with the new technology. And are you really going to use an indicator? That's so . . . déclassé. And your hat . . . you look like Bette Davis in that. And don't get me started on your truck . . . it smells like PBR, Swisher Sweets, and cheap floatant."

DID YOU KNOW...

. . . the Izaak Walton League is actually a baseball organization?

. . . only one percent of the all the world's water is habitable for trout, and only one tenth of one percent of that water has fish that are keyed on your pattern?

. . . Ohio is the new New Zealand?

significant others

Women do not, generally speaking, get fishing, particularly fly fishing. I know some do, and I run into women fly fishermen more and more. In the words of a woman named Martha Stewart—who would make an excellent fly fisherman, if she wasn't involved with the sport of gaming various aspects of the SEC code—it's a good thing. However, it has been my personal experience that they view fly fishing as a perplexing waste of time and money. Many wives, while encouraging you to fly fish (or at least not complaining about it), have absolutely no interest whatsoever in learning how to do it. Men beseech them to consider taking up the sport, and it's almost like you suggested that the family buy a Ducati instead of a Prius. They may even accuse you of wasting money on your hobby.

They don't know the half of how much money we fritter away on fly fishing. A friend of mine refers to these expenditures—even trips—as "off the books." I mean, if we actually told our spouses how much a guided trip costs, or how much a rod goes for, I think we'd be pillow-talking to the sofa for a few months.

There is a black-budget aspect to fly fishing that makes U.S. defense spending look like a quick run to 7-Eleven. For example, a halfway decent rod runs $300, and a good one $650. For a rod. Most people I know have about six or seven rods. I think I have seven unbroken rods, two good cane rods, and a couple of Sages I haven't quite gotten around to sending in for repair. Oh, and two glass ones. And a pack rod. Every night, I type "Orvis CFO IV" into the search field on Ebay, just to see what comes up. I've purchased at least one reel and three spools to match the two other CFO IVs that I own already. You know, redundancy, in case I lose the first eight spools I already have in some tragic spool mishap.

Explain that to your wife. Of course, say you had just dumped 50K on a new kitchen. She wouldn't know that you spent at least that much on beadheads alone.

Several women have begged me to take them fly fishing. Fly fishing is an intimate act; a married person does not take a single woman fly fishing, unless you want to be on the business end of a divorce lawyer. I mean, it would be safer for a marriage to just say, "Hey, honey, me and Woman X are going over to The Sports Page for beers and we'll see what the heck happens," than it would be to say you're going fly fishing with another woman.

Other women ask me if I fly fish, and they seem interested or even vaguely impressed, mostly because it seems kind of nurturing and therefore attractive in an androgynous sort of way. I would get the same reaction if I told them I was intensely interested in needlepoint. "You . . . are? Really? Needlepoint (fly fishing)? How . . . sensitive." Yeah, I'm a sensitive guy. Except when I run into someone in my hole.

Then I'm just like a bass fisherman.

"Ask knot . . ." —John Fitzgerald Kennedy

"We will fight them on the beaches if we can't get them into a net. We will never surrender." —Winston Churchill

"A rise is a rise is a rise." —Gertrude Stein

planning your life around fishing

I am often accused by friends of quote, planning your life around fishing, unquote. This is true. Every aspect of my life, every major decision, every trip centers around whether there is fishing nearby, can I get to it, will it cost me anything, and will it be good if I go. I simply refused to interview for several jobs in central to southern California in 1980 because I was pretty sure there wasn't a decent trout stream nearby. Another job I was offered (in a Western state) became problematic because I was quite certain good fly fishing was four hours away. There was nearby salmon and steelhead fishing, but even salmon fishermen will admit that it's very boat-intensive, and boat ownership is simply something I will never engage in again. Owning any boat larger than a driftboat, rowboat, or canoe is one of life's tiresome chores, precisely what I'm trying to avoid when I go fly fishing. So I blew off the new job in the Western state. Another major job I was up for in an industrial Midwestern state, a job that, had I actually gotten it, would have been lucrative in the extreme. But my mind kept coming back to the essential fact: no trout.

I walked into the building, and it went downhill from there. Another major life decision totally influenced by fishing. Even the interview with the editor was laced with my vague yet perceptible hesitation due to the lack of obvious trout streams.

"Why do you want to work here at the (Major Midwestern Pulitzer Prize-Winning Newspaper)?"

"Frankly, I'm not sure that I do," I confessed with stupid honesty. I actually said this. I was running the trout numbers as I answered. Never mind salary, stock options, creative freedom, or any of that ancillary junk. As I was wrapping up the interview, I spent the most amount of time talking to their columnist about where he liked to go fishing. His answer was Colorado, a

place that begins with a C and ends with an O that was not the big city I was in that began with a C and ended with an O.

About the only thing I decided to do without thinking about trout was deciding to get married, and, in retrospect, I probably should have gamed that out a little bit with fly fishing as, at least, a minor factor. One of my best friends in college actually got divorced because his new wife was distressed by the amount of time he was spending on piscatorial pursuit. "I mean, for Christ sake," he once muttered, "she knew I was a fishing writer." Guess she thought she could Change Him, as many women do. You can change drunks, you can change slobs, you can change sports junkies. You can bust them, make them go to church, buy them new wardrobes, and cut them off from sex, but you cannot change a fly fisherman. Period. New graf.

Vehicle decision? "Is it going to work for fly fishing?" House decision? "Is there a place where I can spread out all my fly-tying stuff, my rods, my gear, and my books?" Socializing decision? "If I drive back from the Deschutes and leave at 5:30 P.M., I could, theoretically make a 7:45 P.M. dinner reservation."

. . . the Crimean War was originally a dispute over some guy hogging a good hole?

. . . a man named Albert Shanker is currently serving a life sentence at a federal correctional facility for poor fly tying?

. . . Mars has water, and the best patterns are extra-terrestrials?

what you think about while you're fishing

I have a job where I get to spend vast amounts of time staring blankly into space with a little trickle of drool hanging out of my mouth. We call this the creative process. Others, of course, naturally assume that you are not, in fact, actually working. When I look like this, I am working. So, when I'm fly fishing, I get to spend even more time by myself, having an internal dialogue with myself about just what idiotic next step I will take with my life. I have an active mind, and my mind does not turn off while I am fishing. When I'm working, I tend to think about Major National Political Issues and the Meaning of the New Hampshire Primary Results and Middle East Peace Roadblocks and stuff like that. I never actually have time to really let my mind wander the way it can when I'm kind of mindlessly stripping in Woolly Buggers. The dialogue usually runs something like this:

"Drag free drift, drag free drift . . . why didn't I go to law school? Mend, mend . . . strip, strip, strip . . . I wonder what that girl I dated for two months in 1978 is doing now? Probably an interior design consultant in Alexandria, Minnesota . . . maybe some floatant . . . the Mariners . . . strip, strip... mend, mend. What should I wear to my high school reunion? There's a rise . . . . that's a good rise over there . . . I miss White Castle hamburgers sometimes . . . cover that little dimple . . . Helena Bonham Carter . . . lousy cast, probably spooked him . . . the 1991 Twins . . . change flies . . . garage needs to be cleaned . . . strip, strip . . ."

And so forth. I have a friend who asserts that he thinks about women while he's fly fishing and thinks about fly fishing when he's with women. I think there's a lot of truth to that. There is an inevitable Larger Meaning to fly fishing, which has been fully explored

in numerous literary fly fishing books, most of which are so precious that they make you want to quit fly fishing for a brief time after you've read them. Still, the authors have made a valid point, and that is that the greater questions can sometimes be answered simply by wandering around a river for a couple of hours flexing a long piece of machined graphite.

I have made several life decisions while on fly fishing trips, and I can tell you they have been better ones than I have made while sitting in traffic or having a couple of drinks in a bar. Mostly, what you think about when you're fly fishing is no more important than what the trout is thinking. You're thinking about the next fly drift, and he's thinking about the next fly drift.

But, the truth must be told here. I usually think about the kind of rod I'm going to get next.

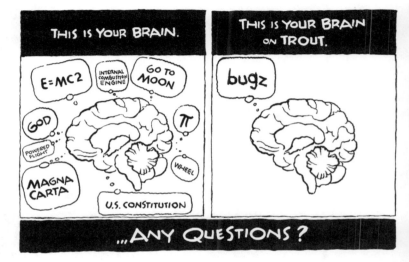

. . . a little-known breed of poodle was bred as a fly-fishing dog, and no one wanted it?

. . . fly fishing is the least popular hobby in Saudi Arabia?

. . . there is no performance-enhancing fly-fishing drug?

etiquette

Not long ago, I was fishing a small creek not far from Ketchum, Idaho. It was a stretch of water perhaps thirty feet across, right next to the road, and heavily canopied. It also had about two hundred rainbows working along the bank. Pretty amazing. It was a one-person situation, trust me.

Seconds after I began casting, squatting like a catcher, four younger guys came blasting up in their dad's SUV. They were from Washington, and I hope one of you jerks happens to buy this book and read this. One guy came right up to me, waded in front of me, balanced precariously on a log ten feet away, and started throwing on my fish. Three others clomped across this beautiful, placid stretch, lit cigarettes, drank their frosty MGDs (you do not drink beer and fly fish—you may, however, drink Scotch and fly fish) and generally shattered my moment. Being the first child that I am, I dislike these types of confrontations, so I didn't scream at the top of my lungs as I should

have. I just caught fish with a size 20 midge while they threw their size 6 Chernobyl Ants or Sofa Pillows at ten-inchers. Morons. It was really the only proper response, other than second-degree murder. They caught nothing. I left.

I then went to dinner with friends and described the situation. One friend, who is intense and therefore a model fly fisherman, asserted with extreme credibility that he would have given them the what-for. Had he had a 9mm, they would all be very badly injured. I noted that Idaho law forbade that sort of thing (I think) and that a tire iron would have been sufficient.

Another friend of mine, an expert guide in eastern Oregon, told me about a time a man wearing a Federation of Fly Fishers logo on his vest, which described him as an officer in that group, jumped into a hole the guide was fishing. The Guide Friend, a large man, noted that the Officer had breached etiquette, and should move on. Lacking basic life survival skills, the

Officer ignored him. The Guide Friend pressed his case forthrightly, and the Officer continued to ignore his very astute observations about his behavior. The Guide Friend and his friend then proceeded to leave their hole and went up to the Officer's SUV. They then let all the air out of his tires, along with a strongly worded letter attached to his windshield. Now, I am not suggesting this is right. It is not. But, in the words of the late, great Sam Kinison, I can understand it.

I have been known to give fellow fishermen an extra two miles of space just so that I don't have to see if they're armed. In the West, you have the luxury of space like that. Back East, etiquette is not just tea-party manners, it's almost mandatory because you can get stuck in the nostril with a backcast.

That hurts almost as bad as a tire iron.

"Speak softly and carry a ten foot for an eight weight."
—THEODORE ROOSEVELT

"The only thing we have to fear is taking a leader out of a package." —FRANKLIN DELANO ROOSEVELT

"Either that fly pattern goes, or I do." —OSCAR WILDE

news stories from the world of fly fishing

Fly Goods Up, CBO Report Says

WASHINGTON, D.C. (AP)--The Congressional Budget Office released figures today showing that fly-fishing purchases surpassed the federal budget.

"There was softness in the retractable-zinger sector, but small tufts of ostrich showed remarkable gains," a spokesman said at a lightly attended news conference in a tributary of the Potomac River.

National defense spending, transfer payments such as Social Security and Medicare, and transportation infrastructure costs slipped behind weird little nippers, elk hair, and titanium bead heads.

New How-To Fly-Fishing Book Is Released; Covers Reeling Techniques, Methods, Tricks

ARCANAE, VT (PR Newswire)--Swampgas Publishers has published the forthcoming book, *Get Reel: 101 Reeling Tips and Strategies,* with an advance press run of 125,000 copies.

"There is an insatiable demand for a book that deals strictly with fly reels and their proper usage," Swampgas president C. Heep Pflueger said. "While thousands of fly fishermen view a fly reel as a minor part of their fishing technique, this groundbreaking new book shows that reels, used correctly, can maximize trout catches exponentially."

Chapters include "Proper Adjustment of Those Little Screws on the Reel Seat," "The First Scratch on Your Peerless and the Devastating Aftermath," "Custom Reel Cozies For Under $200," and "How to Remember to Reset the Drag When a 19-inch Trout is Stripping Faster Than Britney Spears."

Bass Fishing Insurgents Make Gains in West, CIA Asserts; Large Colorful Boats with GPS Scare Off Wary Fly Anglers

DRIBBLE, OR (AP)--Rising tensions between bass fishermen with big, scary boats and fly fishermen with only waders have reached crisis proportions, a CIA study says.

"Massive fiberglass bass boats with three separate engines burning six gallons of fuel per second have forced local fly anglers back into the hills," said a CIA analyst who asked to remain anonymous. "These fly fishermen, who only have Gore-Tex and neoprene, can't compete with the technology and firepower these bass guys have," he added.

A leader of the fly fishing forces read a statement broadcast on shortwave radio declaring that the band would regroup.

"Some of the guys have inflatable float tubes and one of them says he can borrow his wife's kayak," the leader said, but expressed pessimism about the outcome.

"We hit one of the bass boats with a cane rod, but it snapped like a twig."

House, Senate Conferees Close to Agreement on "No Fly Fisherman Left Behind" Legislation

WASHINGTON, D.C. (Reuters)--Congressional leaders expressed optimism Thursday that a bill designed to subsidize fly fishermen making under three million dollars per year will pass both houses narrowly.

"Now all disadvantaged American fly fishermen can have a fighting chance at owning and using equipment that's available to the top wealthiest one percent of all U.S. fly fishermen," Sen. Christopher Dodd (D-CT) said.

"When I see an average working fly fisherman using two-piece rods that are ten years old, it brings a tear to my eye," Sen. Russ Feingold (D-WI) noted, and he pledged to add an additional $21 billion to the request.

"With this $1.8 trillion bill, another 28 percent of all fly fishermen will be able to fish Winston rods with Bauer reels, and that is good news for America," Feingold added.

The White House had no official response, but has agreed that the War on Terror will have to be put aside so that more fly fishermen can be properly outfitted, a senior Administration spokesman said.

Local Man Berated in Wyoming Fly Shop When He Called a Fly Rod a "Pole"

PISCES FLATS, WYOMING (AP)--A middle-aged man was mercilessly berated Monday when he walked into a high-end fly shop and asked if they had any "fly-fishing lures."

Adipose County sheriff's deputies immediately seized the man, who was cuffed and questioned.

Released on bail, the man said he was merely a tourist passing through when he decided to go into the shop and "see what all the hullabaloo about fly fishing was about."

The store's owner, who asked not to be identified, said this sort of thing happens all the time, and that "it's a sad commentary when someone comes in and uses improper terminology."

Other store patrons confirmed the account, and said the man interrupted a heated conversation about the buoyancy of peacock herl.

"Tensions were running pretty high, I guess, and this jackass comes in and just . . . ! don't know . . . wrecks the mood."

Girlfriend Asks Beau to Teach Her to Fly Fish for the 12,893 Time

BARAGA, MI (AP)--It wasn't the first time Susan Drakulich asked.

"I can't teach her how to fly cast, let alone anything else like that—knots, whatever," her exasperated boyfriend Paul Henley, a 29-year-old electrician, exploded over beers in a picturesque tavern just out of town on U.S. Route 41.

"I mean, I can barely double-haul. She'll see how crappy I am at fly fishing and think I'm incompetent. I still haven't gotten the clinch knot down—I have to look at that little knot guide in the new line box they always give you. It would be devastating to me and to her," Henley said.

For her part, Ms. Drakulich, a 27-year-old waitress, notes that she only "wants to share something fun" with her boyfriend of eight months.

Henley vehemently objected, saying, "The next thing you know, she'll be wanting to learn how to tie flies, and I am, like, totally lousy at post wings, still."

NASA Mars-Probe Photographs Indicate Water Present, Slow Hatches, and Picky Feeding "Fish"

JOHNSON SPACE CENTER, TEXAS (AP)--Mission Control flight engineers are puzzling over a series of photos that seem to indicate not only water on Mars, but also lousy hatches and picky "fish."

"Well, I would say that this is a little beyond what we had thought. Many of us posited water as a possibility on Mars, but the bad hatch and weirdly selective fish-like creatures are a complete surprise," said NASA spokesman Bugs Algone.

The computer-enhanced imaging system shows meandering rivers that "look great" but are filled with picky, tentacled, slimy creatures that dive to the bottom the first time you blow a cast, very much like Earth's trout. And, like trout on this planet, Mars's "trout" are maddeningly finicky.

One hapless extraterrestrial fisherman, who had just switched to 8X and a size 26 Brassie had his mothership blow up the planet.

NASA flight controllers were speechless as the Red Planet and its rivers exploded in a blue flash, but said they understood the feeling.

No further Mars missions are scheduled.

Man Who Acts Like He Knows Everything About Fly Fishing Is Skunked

BORINGMAN, MT (AP)--A local fly-fishing blowhard was skunked today after bragging that he could make a seventy-foot cast followed by a drag-free drift.

The man, who was unidentified, is a regular at the local fly shop, area residents say, and he is well known for his high-minded pronouncements and quasi-scientific sounding BS.

"I can't stand him," said Pierce Weippe, a 67-year-old angler.

"He's always in here, telling us all about Hymenoptera and how great they are for trout. Then I pointed out that Hymenoptera is a butterfly," Weippe said.

Weippe also said the man sometimes would pretend to have invented fly patterns.

"He showed me one of them, and it was a Royal Wulff. Guy ain't too swift," Weippe said. "But he's a born liar and you gotta relate to that."

fly-fishing boot camp

I have been around a couple of people—they know who they are—who, when you fish with them, feel compelled to critique your casting. Now, this sort of thing is fine as far as it goes, say, in a situation where that massive rainbow is rolling under a tree seventy feet away, you can't get the line to load right, and maybe your buddy says: "Hey, your shooting line is stuck on your belt buckle."

Other than that, it's usually just irritating to get critiqued while you are actually fishing. Before? Fine. After? Fine. But not during. One friend, who is probably the best caster I know, used to jokingly refer to himself as the Heinrich Himmler Fly-Casting School. Maybe. But I think it's more like Parris Island.

"GOOD MORNING LADIES!"

"SIR, YES, SIR!"

"ARE YEW SMILING AT ME, PRIVATE?"

"SIR, I'M JUST TRYING TO LEARN HOW TO USE THIS FLY POLE, SIR!"

"PRIVATE, DID YEW JUST CALL A FLY ROD A 'POLE'?"

"SIR, YES, SIR!"

"PRIVATE, I WILL PERSONALLY MASH YOUR BARB, CLIP YOUR ADIPOSE FIN, AND TRIM YOUR HACKLE IF YEW EVER CALL A FLY ROD A 'POLE' AGAIN! DO I MAKE MYSELF CLEAR?"

"SIR, I JUST WANT TO LEARN HOW TO CATCH TROUT ON THESE BUGS, SIR!"

"PRIVATE, DID YEW JUST CALL AN INSECT A 'BUG?'"

"SIR, YES, SIR!"

"GODDAMMIT, PRIVATE, A BUG IS A SPECIFIC TYPE OF CREATURE THAT IS NOT TAXONOMICALLY AN INSECT! DEW YEW READ ME?"

"SIR, YES, SIR!"

"PRIVATE, REPEAT AFTER ME: THIS IS MY FLY ROD, THIS IS MY POLE! ONE IS FOR ANGLING, THE OTHER'S FOR . . ."

the log: a year of fishing dangerously

Many of our more fanatical fly-fishing peers keep a log. East Coast fishermen usually refer to it as a journal, particularly if they have master's degrees in English Lit. I have a log for one river, but I am so slothful that I can barely keep up with it the one time a year I write in it. I can't even find it now. Of course, the first year you make notations in it, they're very elaborate:

"September 12, 1998. The sun-kissed waters gently lapped against the verdant bank as the speckled trout sipped gamely at Callibaetis. Overhead, a red-tailed hawk screeched as he circled warily, an avian AWACS searching for the moment to strike the unsuspecting . . ."

Ten years later, notations usually read more like this:

"9/17/2007—caught one 8-inchr on bl. w. olv w/ 6x lost 2, cold as hell went bck to camp had three Jack n cokes /scrw it"

The following may well be an actual log from 2008:

January 24. *Tried Deschutes, just for the hell of it. Rained the whole time. Turned three fish in eight hours. Broke Sage six weight ($695) and skinned back of hand wide open on rock. Snowed all the way on the pass back to Portland. Jack-knifed semi on highway.*

February 18. *Went to Deschutes and broke off about sixteen flies in two hours. Slipped on submerged rocks like greased bowling balls in Crisco. Lost reading glasses on trail. No takes. Hooked myself in ear. Got flat in Redmond. Couldn't find Powerbars in back. Ate old*

Fly Fishing Log
Year One

The Big Sasquatch River (mile 7)   Page 178

May 8 - What a stunning day! Air temp: 58
Wind SSE @ 2-5 mph with light
scattered cloudiness, which makes the light
conditions perfect. The majestic Douglas
Firs frame a magnificent pale cerulean
blue sky (cielo in Español!). I quickly
tied on a size 16 parachute Adams on a
6x Maxima knotted leader, in order to
cover a feisty 14 inch German Brown
(Latin name: Salmo trutta). The light yellow
and deep crimson spots flash as the fish
is brought to my hand; the soft buttery color
of the temporarily defeated adversary is
stupendous; a palette of saffron contrasting
with the mocha back. I return my finny foe,
admiring the glinting waters as they
cascade inexorably to the mighty Pacific
Ocean. Water, which is composed of two parts
Hydrogen and one part Oxygen, is also common

Fly Fishing Log
Year Two

B-S RIVER   5-8

CAUGHT FOUR ON
BIG BLACK WOOLLY
AT MILE 7 BY ROCK
SHAPED LIKE
VOLKSWAGON BUG

Tee Many Martoonies!

french fries off floor. Couldn't get any radio stations that didn't have Classic Country Hits of the Eighties.

March 20. *Was two hours late leaving Portland because I forgot to buy new boots. Stopped at three fly shops to find right-size boot. They didn't have any, so I bought a size 13 ½. I wear an 11. Got to river and immediately fell in. Dropped rod in current, with new reel. Had back-up rod in Tahoe but no reel.*

April 29. *Drove to Deschutes to hit March Browns. Realized it was April. Left box with all my March Browns in Portland. Caught one 9-incher on Woolly Bugger. Ran out of 6X. Very sunny, got burned because I forgot suntan lotion. Used peanut butter instead.*

May 8. *Tried Deschutes again. Stopped by Wasco County sheriff going 91 in 55. $178 fine. Went to favorite spot by guardrail and slipped down embankment. Broke new Winston rod at handle. Fortunately remembered to bring spare rod and reel, but the spool had full sink line on it. Caught two 10-inchers on Woolly Bugger. Forgot to bring lunch. Tried some berries on nearby bushes. I don't feel that great now.*

June 12. *Salmonfly hatch!!! Went to Maupin and there were about 378 guys in each hole. Wedged my way into a spot and got into verbal altercation with fellow angler. He asked me if "I wanted to go, bitch?" I declined. Went back to Tahoe and drove up to secret spot by barbed wire fence. Almost stepped on a rattler on rock, but got out of the way just in time. Realized I left box of Stimulators I had tied in garage. Got down to water, and tied on every fly I had in the box: nothing. Then I tied on a #22 Cream Midge and hooked a 21-incher on 7X. Broke off in three seconds. Walked back to car. Cried a little.*

July 17. *Drove to Ketchum and fished Big Wood with friend. Friend caught 85 or so. I kept striking too hard and broke off three. Had $120 dinner. Drank most of a bottle of red wine too fast and was pretty sick. Friend put me to bed. Woke up next morning with bad headache. Too sick to fish. Sat in car while friend caught 95 up to 22 inches. Drove home.*

August 8. *Went up to mountain lake off Pacific Crest Trail. Twisted ankle on way up. Found a good walking stick and made it to lake. Made camp. HUGE thun-*

derstorm. 60 mph gusts. Made three casts. Went back to car. Lots of cattle around. One of them ate my mirror off. One tire flat (sharp gravel). No cell coverage. When I got back there was letter from IRS.

September 16. Drove up to Idaho with friend. Got into argument over tippet material; he sulked for 200 miles. Wouldn't talk to me for three hours, then asked me if "I wanted to go, bitch." Declined. Left vest in Portland, had to borrow a bunch of gear and flies from friend. Still sulking. Caught 100 cutts, all 11 inches.

October 21. Went up to Deschutes and actually hit a spinner fall. No spinners in box. Must have been 600 fish rising within a hundred yards. Tried to think of a way to fake a spinner. Ripped hackles of flies, tried to mash down wings, no luck. Went back to car (one and quarter miles), found spinners, ran back (15 minutes, not bad for 47). Minor chest pains, light headed. Note to self: make doctor appointment.

November 2. Tried Deschutes. Absolutely nothing. No hatch, no rises, no takes, no molecular motion. Biologically dead. Tried all flies and got nowhere. Must have tied on new dropper every fifteen minutes. Used up all tippet material.

December 3. Went to Deschutes. Tied on Mepps spinner with fat nightcrawler. Limited out on 18-inchers. Yay!

... the preferred food of trout is actually Hot Pockets?

... the money spent on fly rods in any given year could balance the federal budget in nine days?

... on average, cats eat more fly-tying materials than trout do per year?

little-known state fly-fishing regulations

Given the fact that we are a federalist system, and that states have the power to regulate things that the federal government doesn't really have an active interest in (other than handing money over to oil companies and defense contractors), each individual state has the power to make fly-fishing law. I have often wondered what those natural resource committee hearings in the state legislatures are like when fly fishing comes up; I mean, does some state senator get really upset when some other state senator introduces a bill to make sure that barbless hooks are used on a certain stretch of river?

State Senator Hogsnag: "Mr. President, I rise in vehement opposition to Mile 4 through 6 on the Little Numb Butt River being designated as a barbless section. It abrogates the very foundations of the U.S. Constitution, desecrates the Magna Carta, and makes a mockery of not only English Common Law, but of the Napoleonic Code."

State Senator Bugflick: "Does the distinguished gentleman rise in support of the wholesale slaughter of thousands of innocent trout, a pogrom against the least among us, a veritable gangland-style execution of . . . ?"

And so on.

So, anyway, the states get to write trout regs. Here are some obscure laws that I am almost positive are on the books.

Wyoming

It is legal to make disparaging remarks about straw cowboy hats on any visiting fly anglers who live in the state of New York, New Jersey, Massachusetts, or Connecticut.

Idaho

It is unlawful to snag another out-of-state fly angler in the head within fifty (50) feet of the offending angler. Outside of a distance of fifty feet, it is considered a competitive sport.

Colorado

It is required that all (all) out-of-state fly anglers wear a colorful bandana around their necks for easy identification.

Utah

Fly angling is defined as "any use of nonmeat-based gear."

Oregon

Any fly angler who complains about the rain may be subject to a $2,200 fine and a state police escort to the California and/or Nevada border.

Washington

Any out-of-state fly angler who deliberately mispronounces for humorous effect the name of the rivers Skookumchuck, Nooksack, Snohomish, Snoqualmie, Puyallup, Sammamish, Duckabush, Dosewallips, Bug Quilcene, Pysht, Ozette, Sekiu, Hoh, Solleks, Sol Duc, Dickey, Queets, Humptulips, Wynoochee, Satsop, Cowlitz, Ohanapecosh, Klickitat, Napeequa, Twisp, Nespelem, and Bumping may be subject to a sensitivity diversion program and/or up to two months in prison.

Montana

It is unlawful to wear and/or use gear on your person, while fly fishing, that has a total value of less than five (5) thousand dollars.

Ohio

Catching any genetically testable trout while in the state of Ohio should immediately be reported to a state game and fish officer, as it must have been an accident.

New Jersey

Any fly angler who physically touches, bumps, impedes, accidentally hooks, impales, snags, snares, jostles, or shoves any other fly angler on Opening Day should expect that sort of thing.

New York

It is unlawful to falsely claim to others that a Long Island Trout is an actual trout.

California

It is unlawful to be in possession of more than two (2) wrecked shopping carts while fishing in the Los Angeles River.

Massachusetts

It is unlawful to compulsively accumulate merchandise from Orvis or any other fly-fishing retailers and not use it for more than a period of ten (10) years, and then run around always telling people you're an actual fly fisherman, when, in fact, you're just an obsessive-compulsive hoarder.

Michigan

Any fly angler who willfully misleads another fly angler about what fly pattern he is using while in the process of landing a fish shall be subject to arrest.

Illinois

Any rainbow trout caught in the Chicago River on a dry fly would be the first since Abraham Lincoln was trying to rack up 2,100 billable hours a year, and shall be featured on all major Chicago TV news stations when they do that weird-but-true funny story at the end of the broadcast and the anchors chuckle before they go to Leno, Letterman, and Nightline.

Connecticut

Fly anglers who are employed by firms in downtown Manhattan are allowed one half hour (1/2) of wistful staring out the window of their commuter train as they contemplate chucking everything and moving to any western state and becoming trout fishing hermits living in a trailer.

Minnesota

Any fly angler who complains to another fly angler that a muskie ate his trout like an anchovy as he was reeling it in shall be subject to: a) $250 fine and b) derisive laughter and c) the phrase, "Well now, geez, ya know, that sorta thing's gonna happen there once in a while, ya know, then."

the guy who is always better than you are . . .

I hate it when someone is better than I am at anything, and an unfortunate rule of life is that there is always someone better than you are. I have often wondered who the second-best neurosurgeon in the United States is, and whether he knows he or she is the second-best. Same deal with fly fishing: you know that when you go fishing in a group, there is this one guy who is better. Sometimes, he could be luckier, or more skilled at reading water, or a better caster, or better at fly selection. I once hurt one of my best friend's feelings because I went off on this rant about how he, at age 54, should actually read some books about flies sometime (he had only been a fly fisherman for fifteen years or so). He has a Ph.D., and he's not used to being lectured. I was being a fly-fishing jerk. I hated myself. He catches more fish than I do all the time, so I wasn't holding myself up as an example of Being Better. Except at identifying fly patterns.

I suppose you could divide up the pool of people who are better than you are into a few subgroupings:

He's better than you are, but doesn't care. I have a few friends like this. They're older guys, around my dad's age, but they really don't act like it's that big of a deal. Mostly, they have pretty low-end gear, smell kind of funky in a Carmex/Swisher Sweet/beer sort of way, and seem to have some weird inner ear thing that makes them know precisely where all the fish are. You can learn a lot from these guys because you haven't strangled them.

He's better than you are, and wants to keep it that way. Almost always suffering from some end-stage trout-based megalomania, these guys want to make

secretly sure that not only do you not do as well as they do, but want to help assure you don't. Fly fishing is stressful enough, and their job is to make sure that not only do you not catch as many fish, but that your experience is made more special by being critiqued constantly. They are expert at putting you in the wrong hole deliberately—"Oh, I'll just fish that crappy water up around the bend."

He's better than you are, but self-sabotages. These guys could be good, but simply don't work hard enough. They start off kicking your ass in the next hole down, catch two decent fish, and then want to take a nap. Maybe they get a little drunk while they fish, or they have a novel they're more into. They are almost more insidious because not only do you catch more than they do, but they then make it immediately clear that you really shouldn't turn it all into a competition.

He's better than you are, but never actually goes fishing. Has a big job at a law firm or a clinic. Has all the stuff, has pictures of nice fish on his wall taken in the early 1990s, knows how to tie an Albright Knot, and can wax eloquently about how to spread the wings when tying a Trico pattern. You call him to go, and he's always got a conference in Chicago that weekend. But, he wants you to call him and give him a full report after.

He's better than you are, except at catching fish. Rod builders. Expert fly tyers. Brilliant casters. Amateur entomologists. Great water readers. Incredible skill sets, which then never translate into actually catching fish.

. . . Apple has scrapped plans for an iRod?

. . . there is a Graduate School of Line Management at the University of Montana?

. . . the main ingredient in fly line is bubble gum?

fly-fishing danger

Snakes

If you fish in the West, you have likely met up with a rattlesnake. Most people I know who have fished the Deschutes, for example, have stepped on a snake, come very close to a snake, sat down next to a snake, almost grabbed a snake when climbing up a hill, heard a snake, or otherwise had a close encounter of the snake kind. I have a friend whose father had one strike at him on the Crooked River in Oregon and had the snake hanging off his pants. Of course, this is a fisherman we're talking about, and, uh, poetic license may have been involved. Good strategies for dealing with a snake include keeping a shovel with you in your fly vest in order to beat it to death. You can hang a fairly good sized shovel on a zinger. Speaking of which . . .

Zingers

Although they look harmless, they have been known to whip people (me) in the face (forceps on cheek after catching an arm while casting). Ow. But they're nowhere near as bad as a . . .

Net on a Piece of Elastic Rope

Most fishermen I know now do not use nets. I stopped about twenty years ago and try to barely touch the trout when I bring it in. But when I was a kid, I always had a net handy in order to subdue the eight-inch browns I would catch in Wisconsin. Wisconsin is brushy, and more than once I have caught the net on a branch, continued to walk, and then been hit with the net square in the shoulder blade at ninety miles an hour. And, if you're fishing around brush, there are . . .

Mosquitoes

The little buggers practically ruined a trip to Idaho last year. I mean, you could put all the Deet on the planet on any exposed skin, and they still managed to find some skin underneath your watch, or sneak into your

ear, or nostril, or . . . anywhere. I had mosquito bites on mosquito bites. I had five bites over one of my eyes, and I had the appearance of going through a thorough session of questioning by Colombian drug lords. And speaking of pain . . .

Accidental Impaling

Ears. Neck. Fingers. My son's head. All of these things have been hooked in some form or another. In Minnesota, if you got a hook jammed in someplace, it was usually big enough to bring up the Titanic. Lure fishermen know how to get a big hook out: cut the barb and point off, and back it up. The smaller fly hooks are more insidious. They don't go all the way through, and you have to really game out an exit strategy. Ripping is the usual route, but tearing is also an option. And, finally, there are . . .

Trout Bites

Trout bites are, granted, not as severe as, say, being on the business end of a Northern Pike (a prehistorically large Midwestern game fish/snake with teeth the size of and as sharp as a good set of Henckel knives). But if you grab a good-size trout by the lower jaw, you're looking at a symmetrical row of bleeding puncture wounds. Happy fishing.

. . . the best known celebrity fly fisherman is Gallagher?

. . . roosters are very unhappy about being the number-one supplier of fly tying material?

. . . the Omnibus Fly-Fisherman-Gear Cost-Relief Act of 2008 died in the House Ways and Means Committee, again?

snags

One of the universal experiences of fly fishing is snags. I haven't really given a lot of thought about this until now, but there are a million ways to get hung up in the naked stream. If you think about it, unless you're fishing dry on a lake, you spend an astronomical amount of time either getting snagged, being snagged, avoiding getting snagged, or recovering from a snag. You spend way more time dealing with snags than you do actually hooking or reeling in fish. Realistically, one should say, "Hey! Wanna go snagging this weekend?", but it doesn't sound like as much fun as going fishing.

There are two types of snagging: in the water and out of the water. Out-of-the-water snags are, usually, quite spectacular and will allow you to waste vast amounts of time attempting to untangle the snag. On Oregon's Crooked River, where I do a lot of fishing, the only real bank obstructions are these bizarre cattaillike plants that are actually spiky instead of nice and fuzzy like regular cattails. They're called tules. When you get hung up on one of these *Star Trek* TV Show Planet flora, you can count on screwing with it for a half hour at least. The tippet seems to be physically consumed by the prickers, forming a cat's cradle from hell that can injure you with tiny scratches.

Snags in overhanging branches are the most common out-of-the-water snags, and are deceptive because you can see them easily. And, many times, you can make a valiant attempt to rescue your fly, if you're lucky. In Idaho, I once hung from a lower branch, on my side of the river, in current, doing a George of the Jungle impression to lurch up to the upper branch where my (very large) Woolly Bugger was impaled. I made the pull-up to the upper branch, which then broke off with the (very large) fly in it. It whipped into my index finger at Mach 2, puncturing my finger.

There Will Be Blood. Ouch.

Branch snags across the stream: forget it. Of course, I have semi-swam over to the other side to get a two-

dollar fly because it was my last Deer Hair Spider Emerger, or whatever it was. You make a few desultory attempts to yank it out, but this only digs the barb in even deeper, and it's usually formed an intricate web of 6X by that point.

Underwater snags will almost invariably lead me to make a try for it. You know the drill: you first pull on it, thinking it's on a rotten twig or a loose piece of bark. Nothing. Then you do the old walk-down-below-it maneuver, which is almost always fruitless. One time, while fishing in the Big Wood River in Idaho, I had an underwater snag. If you fish a high traffic area, you have had the experience of picking up a fishing line or leader underwater. I was using a size 12 hopper and an 18 Copper John dropper. I yank on the line, it comes out, and I reel in my size 12 hopper and 18-inch Copper John dropper, which has a size 12 hopper and an 18 Copper John dropper entangled in it. Of course I used it after I lost my rig on a snag. And then it got snagged. I quit.

TROUT "!" QUOTES

"Fly fishing is ninety nine percent irritation and one percent imitation" —THOMAS A. EDISON

"Rarely is the question asked: Is our children fishing?" —GEORGE W. BUSH

"Neither a borrower of flies nor a lender be." —WILLIAM SHAKESPEARE

what guides say, what guides mean

Guides Say	Guides Mean
"Have you ever been fly fishing before?"	"You obviously have never been fly fishing before."
"Where you from?"	"I don't care where you're from."
"If you have any questions, feel free to ask."	"Shut the hell up, hold this rod, and I will tell you precisely what to do, and you will do precisely what I tell you to do when I tell you to do it."
"Oh, you're a fly fisherman. Good!"	"Your wife got you a rod in a desperate bid to get you out of the house."
"Nice hat!"	"What a stupid hat!"
"Tie on this pattern for starters."	"You look like a moron, and you clearly can't figure this out yourself."
"Look, there's a rise!"	"Christ, are you blind? RIGHT THERE!"
"I like to use this leader material."	"That's the stuff that looks like the line on your Snoopy Zebco."
"No, put the fly over there."	"Not in the tree, idiot. The water. The water."
"These aren't ideal conditions."	"Prepare to write a $350 check for a boat ride."
"It's only 50 feet. Double-haul."	"TEN AND TWO!!! GOD!!! IT'S NOT BRAIN SURGERY."

Guides Say	Guides Mean
"Right over there, behind the rock."	"Like you can make that cast."
"Oooh! That was a close one!"	"Um, next time, don't play it like a tuna."
"I like it a little cloudy."	"Put on your rain gear."
"Here. Let me tie it on for you."	"Spaz."
"NICE fish!!!"	"Thank GOD. FINALLY!"
"Okay, don't horse him in."	"Three . . . two . . . one . . . BUSTED LEADER."
"A gourmet lunch is included."	"Do you like Spam?"
"See that riffle? Wade right over there."	"I can hardly wait to see you go ass over teacups."
"Wow! That's another nice 22-incher!"	"Wow! Thanks for the $100 tip!"
"No, don't pick him up like that."	"He's dead."
"No, sir, we can't keep any to eat."	"I would like to personally put this live, flopping trout in your mouth now."
"You're really improving!"	"I am amazed by my ability to lie so brazenly. I think I will run for the U.S. Senate."
"GREAT cast."	"Gee. It went straight."
"That's what we call a Blue Wing Olive."	"JESUS Christ. IT'S NOT A BUG!!!"
"Thanks, what a great day!"	"I'm quitting and going back to get my fourth master's."

fly-fishing clubs

Given that mankind is always taken with social organization, it was inevitable that fly fishermen would band together to form fly-fishing clubs. I have never joined a fly-fishing club; most of the ones I know serve valid functions, like having a comfortable place to pathologically lie to other pathological liars while pathologically drinking. Okay, that's a little harsh. They throw in a little stream restoration work on the side.

I should probably join the local fly-fishing club. I once went to a meeting and gave a little talk about . . . hmm . . . I guess it was fly fishing. That's all they seem to talk about. I did hear a lot about Lipitor, too (yeah, I take it, 10 mgs, so I'm not being all holier-than-thou). They have a president, a vice president, a recording secretary, a treasurer, and a Minister of Propaganda. Oh, and a small paramilitary force. Okay, they have all but one of those. They also have minutes taken. What the heck kind of minutes you would want to take at a fly-fishing club that anyone would want to read or save is beyond me:

"President calls meeting to order. Calls upon recording secretary to read minutes of previous meeting. Motion is made and seconded to dispense with reading of minutes, except for the part about the resolution strongly condemning the use of Flashabou as unsporting and too much like a bass lure. Motion passed."

But there's always a newsletter.

Neoprene County Fly Fishers Club Newsletter

"All the Neoprene County Fly Fishing News That's Fish to Print"

June Edition No. 78

Welcome from the President!

Greetings fellow anglers! We had a great meeting at the Neoprene County Convention Center at the new Motel Six on Rte 237.

While there was the usual amount of extremely heavy drinking, I would like to caution members that "fish"-ticuffs over natural fur vs. poly blend dubbing material is "taking things too far." The Neoprene County Attorney's Office informs me that they will not seek to press charges if members will compensate the management. Let's pony (or trout!) up, people ! ;-)

As your president, I am pleased to announce that the "State of the Club" is on the "rise!" Let's make it a "striking"-ly good year!

Tight lines,

Mike Crodrag, NCFFC

Treasurer's Report

The NCFFC is in good financial shape. I think we have about seventy dollars or thereabouts. I need to check. I put the money in my truck. My son's been driving it around, so I can't guarantee it's still there. I'll ask him.

Respectfully submitted,

Bob

Bob Drift, Treasurer, NCFFC

This Month's Tip...

Next time you're casting to a rising trout, remember to check to see if you still have a fly on. --MC

Hotspots!

Lower Abdomen River--Try using a dry, wet, or nymph right by that one tree, or the rock. It works!

"Fishy Tails Corner"

"I was stripping in a size 6 olive woolly bugger last month at the impoundment, when all of a sudden, my line got hooked on something. It could have been a snag, but I betcha it was probably a pretty nice trout. It could have been, anyway. But there are a lot of old tires in there." -- C.D. See

"Reel"-y Nice Fish!

Here are some nice shots taken of some "big-uns!" from our members--keep 'em coming, guys!

anagrams

For years, one of my avocations was creating anagrams. I would slave for hours coming up with letter juxtapositions to form new original meanings. I would struggle with Bob (Bbo and Obb were all I could come up with—not that great). Then I found an anagram tool online the other night, and I was off to the races. You just plug the phrase or word into the search engine, and in a split second you would have 23 or 589 or 51,111 (yes, that was a real number of possible combinations) different anagrams based on trout stuff.

Hmm.

So I spent an evening doing this instead of something constructive, like getting my taxes ready or rearranging my grizzly hackle capes. For example, I plugged in CADDIS HATCH and out came I'D CATCH SHAD. Sweet. I then typed in GUIDE'S EGO and out came I DO USE EGG. MADISON GUIDE re-formed as A DEMIGOD IN U.S., and, frankly, who could deny their divine status? SNOTTY GUIDE came back as TINY EGO STUD and STUDENT YOGI—now we were getting somewhere.

Some of the anagrams had double meanings or were just funny phrases: NIGHTCRAWLER became LAWN RETCH RIG. INDICATOR came out as NO CIA DIRT. Oh, thank God. BASS GUY morphed into GAY BUSS, the last thing a Bubba would want. TROUT GUY = ORGY TUTU. And so on.

One of my favorites was BAITFISHING = I HIT SNAG, FIB. WHIPFINISH became HIP FISH WIN. RAINBOW turned out to be BAR WINO or BRAIN OW. MUSTAD HOOK was SAD MOUTH OK, and who could disagree with the trout who had a sad mouth from a Mustad? Major rivers such as the DESCHUTES wound up as THESE SCUD, and the FRYING PAN rearranged as FANNY GRIP, which is funny but not descriptive, unless there's more going on at the Pan than meets the eye.

FISHING SCHOOL was IF CON, HIGH LOSS. Yeah, man, those schools can be a con and are expensive. It also was GOSH, FILCH IS ON! Don't tell anyone if you think you're getting robbed. ROYAL WULFF became OR AWFUL FLY and OUR FLY FLAW, not something the pattern's devotees would want to hear. ROLL CAST twisted itself into SCAR TOLL, which is true if you're on the business end of a bad cast. BROOKIE became OK, I BORE, and the mighty CUTTHROAT became the more convivial TROUT CHAT, or, more ominously and like his pursuers: COAT TRUTH.

But the grand finale was LIVE BAIT = A BIT EVIL.

FLY FISHING RECORDS

Largest trout caught on fly purchased in hardware store: Brook trout, 7 inches (September 4, 1968, Carp River, Michigan)

Longest cast made by a dog: three feet, two inches (April 19, 1956, Phydeaux Creek, Idaho)

Number of brown trout caught with a piece of carpet fuzz by an angler after he went through entire fly box: 12 (August 12, 1987, Karastan River, Oregon)

the ten weirdest things that have happened to me while fly fishing

1. A swallow grabbed my caddis on the Deschutes, and I was briefly playing it as it flew twenty feet in the air. Broke off, naturally. Story of my life.

2. A freak hailstorm came in off a canyon rim, and it looked like the leading edge of a nuclear blast. I was pelted by hail that felt like ball bearings. I have pictures.

3. I slipped and fell in the North Fork of the Santiam. My waders filled with water, and I was being swept toward a 20-foot-deep hole. I had no buoyancy to speak of. My friend found a big branch, and I grabbed it just as I was about to go into the hole.

4. I hooked and landed a 19-inch brown in the Fall River. Two days before, I had hooked a really big fish and broke it off. In the 19-inch brown's mouth was my own very distinctive fly I was using two days before.

5. I was once offered an opportunity to fish with Jimmy Carter. I had a prior engagement and stupidly deferred. I have regretted it ever since. I gave him an original cartoon instead, and he wrote me a very nice hand-written note thanking me. I then immediately regretted all the mean cartoons I did about him from 1978–1981.

6. McGeorge Bundy, President Kennedy's National Security adviser, was coming to our editorial board. I was supposed to go on a trip to the Deschutes. I decided in favor of the fishing trip. I caught a nice 17-inch brown, and Bundy died days later. I felt somehow responsible.

7. I once left a fly vest with about $1,500 worth of equipment hanging on a branch as I was taking a leak on a float trip. I forgot the vest. I had to bum flies for three days. I felt like a homeless person. "Spare caddis?" "Will work for nymph."

8. I grabbed a small water snake with a trout in its mouth and freed it. I hate snakes.

9. A cow ate my car mirror off my Nissan 300Z while I was fishing a ranch pond. I was tempted to go tear the tail off the cow for fly-tying material, but then I remembered PETA.

10. I was on a trip to Kelly Creek, and went ahead of my party, which included my dad. They thought I went upstream, and I didn't. They eventually concluded I was dead. When they caught up to me hours later at twilight, my dad was in tears. I had no idea I was dead and said, "What's the matter?" My dad said, "I'm just glad you're alive, son." I said, "I caught twelve, what's the problem?" They made me buy dinner, they were so angry.

fly-fishing magazines

I love fly-fishing magazines even more than I love political journals, mostly because the writers get so exercised about arcane points of minutiae that no outsiders could possibly care about or understand. The letter writers are even worse.

To the Editor:

I note in the January issue that you once again completely and utterly miss the point of titanium bead heads. Anyone with an ounce of sense is fully cognizant of titanium's higher density, and therefore, its faster sink rate. Brass, from a metallurgical standpoint, is vastly inferior. You owe your readers an apology. Cancel my subscription immediately.

Winston Powell Phillipson III
Dredge, VT

And so on.

I have read fly-fishing magazines off and on for thirty years now, and I have developed some preferences. As a rule, they are dramatically less breathless than their bass and other freshwater-variety counterparts. Any given bass magazine is written in the style of the *U.S. Army Special Forces Field Manual*, and stresses the deadly aspects of the sport. I mean, bass fishermen use electronics as a matter of course, and that is antithetical to the relatively low-tech, fur 'n' feathers ethos of the fly fisherman. I assume that any day the bass boys will join forces with the Pentagon and figure out a way to strategically target bass with a Tomahawk cruise missile. Maybe they can paint it chartreuse.

Of course, no fly-fishing magazine is complete without:

- A thoughtful, reflective columnist who manages to extract a Larger Life Lesson from an experience they had with a bottle of fly floatant.

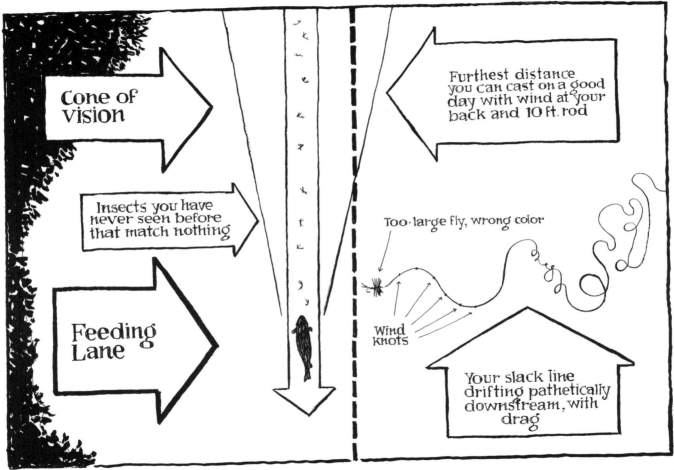

Cone of Vision

Insects you have never seen before that match nothing

Feeding Lane

Furthest distance you can cast on a good day with wind at your back and 10 ft. rod

Too-large fly, wrong color

Wind knots

Your slack line drifting pathetically downstream, with drag

- An article about a new hot spot with four-color maps, suggested fly patterns, and GPS coordinates that also happens to be your favorite, formerly unknown hole.

- Ads for products that are, I think, on some level some sort of practical joke: "Tired of Whip Finishers That Don't Have Digital LED Time Displays?"

- The latest destination resort-country fishing spot of choice: "Burkina Faso: Equatorial Brown Trout Bonanza" or "Saddam's Secret Spots: Nymphing the Tigris and Euphrates."

- Gear reviews: "The New Float-Tube Cozies: Are They a Waste of Money?" "Latest Space Age Technology Proves Fiberglass Rods and Automatic Reels Are the Best After All" "Are Virtual Rods the Wave of the Future?"

TROUT "!" QUOTES

"If you give a man a fish, he will eat for a day; if you teach a man to fly fish, he will starve in about a week."
—ANONYMOUS

"One morning I caught a trout in my waders. How he got into my waders I'll never know." —GROUCHO MARX

"By any means necessary, except San Juan Worms."
—MALCOLM X

sensational fly-fishing magazines

I was flipping through some outdoor magazines while I was getting $291 worth of tires put on the other day. They didn't have any fly-fishing magazines there, but they did have two different outdoor magazines. No, not *Outdoors* magazine, which is kind of like an outdoor magazine if it was put out by *GQ*, but real, blood-and-guts Bubba rags with ads for Skoal and Jack Daniels and Elk Meat Smokers and Big Deadly Knives and rifles that could easily secure the Green Zone. Fly-fishing magazines are not like this. I mean, we fly-fishing types are into feathers. There are no articles about the top five ATVs or the best pistols with which to finish off a grizzly (that would be a cruise missile, actually, and don't miss the first time).

What if fly-fishing magazines adopted the regular-guy outdoor magazine ethos? We'd probably see some articles like these:

"How I Battled a 15-Inch Brookie with a Two-Weight Cane Rod and an 8X Tippet—and Survived."

The regular outdoor magazines are all about surviving. You never see the word "survive" in a fly-fishing magazine.

"Fly-Fishing Retrievers: What's the Best Breed for You?"

It would be cool if there were fly-fishing dogs, like hunting dogs. But they would have to be very aesthetically pleasing.

"Get the Point: Hooks That Rip Lips and Take Names"

Although any serious fly fisherman has had many conversations about hooks (yes, non-fly fishermen, it's true, we talk about stuff like that), you never hear fly

fishermen talk about how to "hook 'em and hold 'em" (remember the Wright and McGill snelled hook packages?). You hear them talking about how to make hooks *safe*, for God's sake. Or not even using hooks at all, like PETA. Bass fishermen pretty much as a rule do not express much remorse about the damage the average bass lure with twelve barbs on it can inflict.

"Ten Best Ways to Get There: What's the Best Fly Fishing SUV?"

Fly fishermen are a little different from bass fishermen, although there is some intersection between the cultures. For example, vehicles. I have a seriously used Chevy Tahoe, a perfectly acceptable regular-guy gas hog. But I also have a Miata, which I am constantly explaining away as a mechanical choice, not a lifestyle choice. Western fly fishermen unapologetically drive big SOB SUVs, for the most part, but there are a lot of Beemers at the trailhead, too. The compromise choice is usually a Subaru Forester or Outback, which has enough room for most of your crap, but also sends the message that You Care. East Coasters tend to use the same car they would use to impress a client. When I see a Hummer at the parking area, I tend to think: low self-esteem.

"Tasty Trout Recipes: Slipping the Brownie on the Barbie"

In my entire life, I have never had a conversation with another fly fisherman about how to prepare a trout to eat, except in the context of a backpacking trip where you're catching lake brookies put there to die at the end of the year, anyway. But the notion of exchanging recipes on how to make a nice brown trout has never passed my lips or that of the hundreds of other fly fishermen I have met. I do have this one friend who says you should eat one trout a year, "just to prove it's not a (expletive deleted) game."

I kind of get that. I don't do it, but I get it.

I just prefer Wendy's.

fly-tying hints

1. Head cement does not make everything better, unless you're accidentally inhaling it.

2. Never confront the fly shop cashier with a tantrum about why a four-inch square of elk ass fuzz costs three dollars. It's not his fault.

3. When borrowing tying material from the bodies of dogs, cats, and parakeets, make sure they're asleep.

4. Flies with simple names (Adams, Coachman, Hendrickson) work better than names you have made up for your own flies (Jack's Classic Rainbow Torpedo Killer Maribou Destroyer Thang).

5. When you start tying flies on the bed in front of your wife or girlfriend at nine at night, the spark is gone.

6. "Why am I wrapping a two-inch piece of chicken feather around a piece of wire the size of a quark?" is a psychological, not an epistemological, question.

7. Fly tying saves money like defense contracting protects America.

8. Do not—repeat, NOT—put a size 20 hook in your mouth to hold it while you gather up the materials upon which to tie it. They really do work, particularly if barbed.

9. Make certain that you do lay out all your tying materials first for a specific pattern, so that when you sneeze, all of it will land in about the same area.

10. A good method of training yourself to become a fly tyer is to first learn how to juggle BBs.

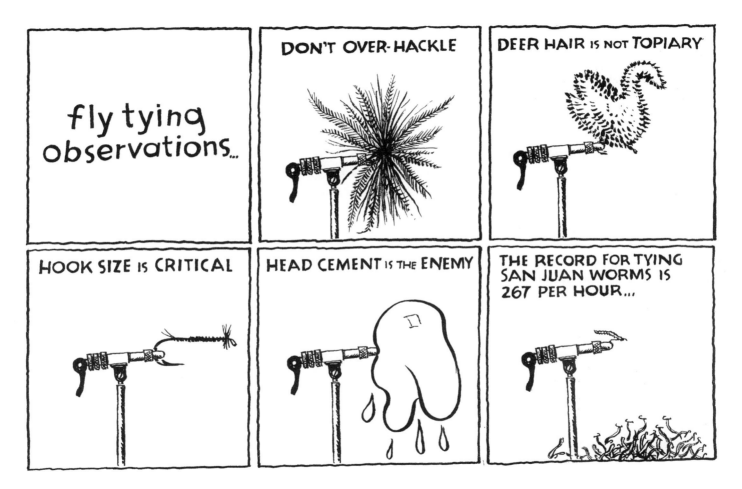

fly tying observations...

DON'T OVER-HACKLE

DEER HAIR IS NOT TOPIARY

HOOK SIZE IS CRITICAL

HEAD CEMENT IS THE ENEMY

THE RECORD FOR TYING SAN JUAN WORMS IS 267 PER HOUR...

trout-fishing video games

I have three children, ages 19, 16, and 13. They all play the usual frightening video games, which probably offer more sensory stimulation than the average Green Drake hatch, so I have a hard time engaging them about fly fishing.

"You mean, you have to stand in the water? Isn't it cold? Couldn't I fall down?"

"Well, yes, I suppose you could."

"And what if I catch something? Do I have to touch the fish? Isn't a fish cold and slimy?"

"Yes, but that's not the point. The point is that you're outside, and . . ."

"Isn't it cold outside sometimes?"

"Again, yes, but . . ."

At this point, they have turned their attention to *Grand Larceny IV: Arraignment Day* or whatever it is that they are playing on the PS2 or XBox 360. There have been actual fly-fishing computer games, and I

have played them in the winter. Not the same, but it's something. Nobody gets shot in the one I play, but we are coming to that. Perhaps, in order to re-engage the next generation in fly fishing, they may develop the following:

U.S. Navy Seals: Operation Blue Ribbon

Join the Seals as they fend off enemy bait fishermen from Barbless-Only stretches of the world's greatest trout streams.

Drift Rage: Get out of My Hole 2

Defeat enemy fly fishermen as they try to sneak into your favorite spot.

Where's Your License? Mashed Barbs III

Evade fish and game wardens as they try to make you dig through your vest, looking for the license you're

almost certain you bought at the gas station in Cheyenne, Wyoming . . . you think.

Shooting Heads: The Final Chapter

Try to destroy Al Qaeda terrorists with nine weights and very heavily weighted nymphs.

Get to the River Before the Other Yuppies: Need for Speed 3

Choose your favorite sportscar and drive like a maniac through insane traffic to claim your spot. No SUVs available.

Number of five ounce glasses of chardonnay consumed by Patagonia-wearing thoracic surgeon after losing a 23-inch rainbow on a 2X tippet: 11

Number of times the phrase "Nice fish!" was said on a half-hour fly-fishing television program: 234 (May 2, 2007, America's Next Top Fly Fishing Idol!)

Most rainbow trout caught while playing harpsichord and double-hauling: 1 (October 23, 1962, D'minor River)

anatomy of a vest

1. 1,489 flies, none of which match any given hatch

2. seven different fly boxes:
   - a Wheatley with a lot of the little windows malfunctioning
   - two cracked plastic boxes from "The Affluent Angler" fly shop
   - two small fly boxes that have a bunch of rusty flies you haven't replaced yet
   - one match box containing four size 24 midges
   - one film canister, empty, but there used to be a few Blue-Winged Olives in there. Or not.

3. 22 leader packages:
   - six have 9 ft., 6X intact leaders, but they were out of the kind you like, so you just grabbed these at a hardware store
   - four are 9 ft., 6X intact leaders, and they are the kind you like
   - twelve empty leader packages

4. three empty tubes of SPF 50 sunblock

5. four empty fly-floatant tubes

6. one 3/4 empty fly-floatant tube

7. one empty tube of that fly-drying stuff you always forget to use

8. three broken zingers with no tool attached

9. one working zinger with all your tools attached, because the other three are broken

10. empty package, Pearson's Nut Goodie, stale

11. empty water bottle

12. calcified half bologna sandwich, still wrapped in Saran Wrap, date unknown

13. those little split shot from England you always forget you have

14. eight tippet material spools, 6X, six of which are rotten

15. one 7X tippet spool, rotten

16. two 5X spools, rotten

17. one 4X, rotten

18. one 3X spool, perfect condition

19. a Scientific Anglers reel spool with full sinking line that goes to a reel you lost

20. a small bag of something you cannot identify

21. a fly hooked immutably in the upper pocket you keep your fly box in, which you always prick your finger on

22. a digital camera with a smashed LCD screen, all other components functioning

23. a hook sharpener you always forget you have

24. a little tool that you bought at the time and forget what it does

25. a nipper with a magnifying glass that you never use, either

26. some little piece of wire that goes to something

27. a AAA battery, dead

28. a Flexlight with no battery

. . . Cheetos make excellent strike indicators?

. . . CNN currently has no programming dedicated to casting?

. . . the Foreign Intelligence Surveillance Act has no enforcement provisions for some stranger asking you what pattern you're using?

fishing tournaments

I am not against bass fishing. Really. I have done a lot of it, enjoy it, and have never caught one more than four pounds or so. But bass are my boyhood fish, so I have a soft spot for them. I still have the Bass-Oreno I got in 1972.

I am against bass fishing tournaments.

Period.

I was watching one of the upper cable channels the other night at about two in the morning (don't ask, this is what single middle-aged men do), and on ESPN 6 or whatever it was, I stumbled across a bass fishing tournament. It was like Roone Arledge meets Izaak Walton.

Fishing shouldn't be stressful. Now, look. I have engaged in a betting pool or two involving fishing. It's good, clean fun. But the whirling graphics, screaming commentary, and, in particular, the garish awards ceremony at the end made me feel like there was no refuge from the utter hideousness of the twenty-first century. It was like the Super Bowl halftime show without the wardrobe malfunction (sadly), with screaming Bass Groupies and Bass Hangers-on and beaming Bass Families and triumphant Bass Gladiators holding their hawgs up by the mouth and unctuous announcers bellowing out the total weight of the catch.

I recall the rather sedate bass-fishing shows of the 1960s and 1970s. There was a friendly, slightly overweight southern host who would run his film (yeah, film), and then, at the end of the show, he would bounce the rig he was using through an aquarium to demonstrate how you used a Texas rig. That was it, usually. That worked for me: low-key, pleasantly tedious, and only about the fishing.

I had a really good friend who was the executive producer of an outdoors show about twenty years ago. He told me they would take live fish along with them, in case the hawg hole wasn't as advertised and there wasn't enough fishin' action. This was not exactly like hearing definitively that there was no Santa Claus, but

let's say it was one of those moments in life when you find out that the nice people who want to give you a free camera actually want you to sit through a pitch for a timeshare.

I like NASCAR, too, but they have NASCARed bass fishing, and the only thing left now is to put logos on the sides of the fish.

Of course, seeing all the fun the bass guys were having with their tournaments, it was not too long before some wiseacre figured out you could have a fly-fishing tournament, too. This is sick and wrong. A little friendly unofficial match between friends is one thing, but making it into some money-making thing is pretty screwed up, in my opinion. There are one-fly tournaments (the least odious of the genre, I suppose), but I did see a show on Channel 998 where someone won a couple of grand and some new gear.

Wait.

I'm in.

"You could get a million fish. I know where they could be gotten, with a spinner. But it would be wrong, that's for sure." —RICHARD M. NIXON

"When you put your hand in the goo that was your fly floatant, you'll know what to do." —GEORGE S. PATTON

"Beware the military-industrial-bass boat complex." —DWIGHT D. EISENHOWER

ask the fly tying troubleshooter

Dear Fly-Tying Troubleshooter:

When stacking elk hair for my favorite caddis pattern (an 18 TDC with an orange dubbed body), I have run into a conundrum. How do I keep ALL the hairs evenly aligned as I pull them out of the hair stacker?
—*TDC Maniac*

Dear TDC Maniac: Forget it. Impossible.

Dear Fly-Tying Troubleshooter:

I have often struggled with the calf-tail post-wing assembly when I'm tying size 16 Adams. I can't get the wing to stand perfectly upright without getting the thread wraps too thick. Help!
—*Stray Calf*

Dear Stray Calf: There's no way to solve it.

Dear Fly-Tying Troubleshooter:

Tying off the head with a whip-finish has always been, for me, a real challenge. When I've tied off the hackle and gotten the wing just right, sometimes the whole fly just kind of blows up right at the end. As I watch the hackle unwind like a kite string and I accidentally cut the bobbin off with the scissors, the wings will spiral into the air like a tiny mushroom cloud. Any advice?
—*Knotless in Seattle*

Dear Knotless in Seattle: You're really screwed.

Dear Fly-Tying Troubleshooter:

For years, I have tied really crappy flies. Thick heads, dry flies that float like the Titanic, nymphs that wind up looking like cigar butts, and Woolly Buggers that look like something out of a 1950s Japanese sci-fi movie. Any thoughts?
—*All Thumbs*

Dear All Thumbs: Yes. Support the Sri Lankan Free Trade Agreement.

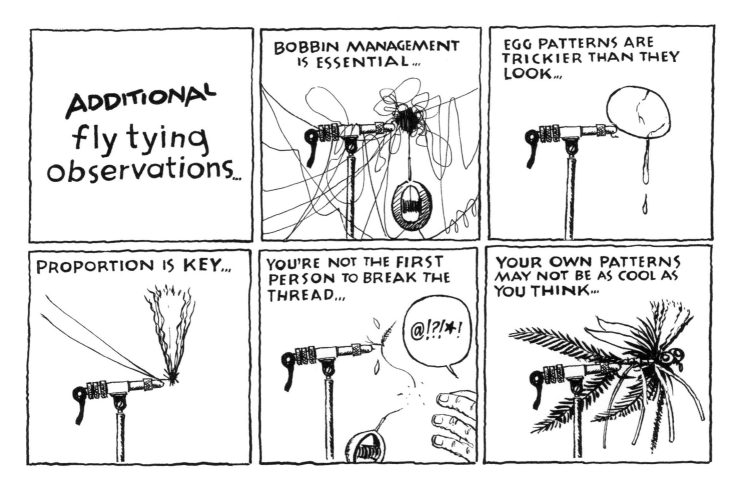

how to talk to other fly fishermen in your spot

Perhaps one of the most vexing problems for many fly fishermen is the notion of maintaining a healthy yet discreet dialogue with fellow anglers who happen to be in your river—or in your spot. Being a naturally convivial person in a sport populated by people who like solitude is a problem. I sometimes feel like Bill Clinton at a Promise Keepers convention when I initiate a streamside chat with another fly fisherman: unwelcome, and yet I press on. The most awkward conversations that I have usually occur at My Spot:

"So, hey. Doing any good?" I chirp in my best faux friendly tenor. You never say "Catching any?" That's so bait.

The Other Guy will usually answer in a fairly cagey manner along the lines of, "Oh, you know. Slow."

"Slow?" Hmm. That's almost always a bald-faced lie. It's what I always say when I'm on My Spot. I am well-known for my truth evasions to other fishermen. I have to assume they're always lying as well. I once stuck my rod in the water completely as a pickup drove by—while I was playing an 18-inch trout—pretending to examine the bottom of a rock. The pickup didn't slow down. Mission accomplished.

"What are you using?" is a personal question, and when asked by strangers, it should not be answered specifically. You could issue responses ranging from "Oh, I'm wet" to the classic, "My own pattern," which is technically true yet wildly nondescriptive. I once told a guy I was using a WMD, and he seemed to think it was a kind of PMD, not a Weapon of Mass Destruction. He nodded, apparently satisfied. Maybe he was a Republican.

Another conversational gambit I employ is inquiring about where the Other Guy is from. In a way, it's not overly personal, but the response can speak volumes about how good the guy is. If he says, "From around here," you're screwed. He has fished your hole 789 times and will be there all day. If he says a city 300 miles away, well, you're in business. He'll move on, because most guys from 300 miles away generally don't know their ass from a hole in the ground. And I have been the guy from 300 miles away more than once.

Sometimes, if you're friendly and the Other Guy is in a good mood, he'll tell you that he is going to another hole. There is this one spot in a small river in Oregon where I would have to watch old guys with automatic reels from the 1950s dredge my water with Mickey Finns. They would confidently announce that they hadn't caught anything, and you weren't going to, either, and sure, come on in, I'm taking off. I would then thank them, compliment them on their automatic reel, and move in to administer the fatal blow.

Occasionally, but not often, the Fellow Angler will be even more voluble than I am, which means he's probably on methamphetamines, and should be avoided.

the fly-fishing school course catalog

As in all arcane pursuits, in order to truly master a subject, one has to go to school. Many fly shops and other retail concerns involving fly fishing offer "fly-fishing schools." Fly-fishing skills and lore used to be passed on from generation to generation, but someone finally figured out how to extract even more money from Upwardly Mobile Fly-Fishing Aspirants by providing a structured, rigorous academic environment. At first, these fly-fishing schools covered basic stuff: casting, reading water, and the usual ancillary topics associated with fly fishing. Now that a master's degree is the floor for many professionals, and the sport has gotten more scientific, a truly dedicated fly fisherman has to keep up. Herewith is the course catalog of a leading fly-fishing school.

TAC 401 MWF 9-10. Principles of Fly-Fishing Tactics. Course covers basic upper division trout-fishing strategies, such as spending $400 on a guide, flying to Patagonia, and sneaking a plastic worm on the shank of your Woolly Bugger while no one is looking.

TAC 402 TuTh 8-9:40. Advanced Principles of Fly-Fishing Tactics. Praying, weeping, wracking sobs, throwing your rod into the river, and therapeutic primal screaming.

ROD 301 MWF 1-2. Theory of Rod Design and Performance. Course examines brand status, color differentiation of graphite relative to casting ability, why there is always a missed guide about three-quarters of the way up the rod, how a size 20 fly can always mirac-

ulously find your scalp on a windy backcast, and why, precisely, your rod tip comes off when playing a fish over 16 inches.

GUI 401/402/403 TuTh 3-4:40. Psychological Underpinnings of Fly-Fishing Guides. Material covered includes why your guide always seems to find fault with everything you do and what motivates him to berate you even though you are paying him more than the hourly wage of a neurosurgeon. Childhood self-esteem issues are explored in relation to why someone who doesn't seem to have a real job most of the time feels comfortable calling a client a "sorry-assed excuse for a fisherman who can't make a 15-foot cast with a piece of yarn and a 3-ounce bullet sinker" and a "whining baby who thinks the fish bite 24/7."

FLY 336 MWF 3-4. Pattern Identification and Entomological Classification of Seemingly Indistinguishable Pieces of Fuzz. Course covers the spectral gradation between the Superfine and natural beaver dubbing olive egg sacs of *Callibaetis* imitations, the aerodynamic properties of parachute hackle, the split-versus post-wing paradox, and the relative buoyancy of elk hair in comparison to deer hair. Upon completion, all students will then be admitted to a mental hospital.

PHI 507 TuTh 1-2:40. Philosophical Antecedents of Ancient Fly-Fishing Conundrums. Class will examine why a leader looks fine in the package and comes out like a Gordian knot, the question of how someone determined Rapalas are morally inferior to a Mickey Finn, why your feet are invariably wet after wearing waterproof boots, and why grotesquely obese bass fishermen always get their own television programs.

eastern fly angling versus western fly angling

As with all other East/West rivalries, both sides have an argument. But with East Coast versus West Coast fly fishing, the West has the upper fin on virtually all levels except for tweediness. I have fished East Coast, Midwest, and Western streams, and I can assure you that the fishing is best in the West. However, the Eastern guys have the usual advantage in these matters, which is tradition. It started in England and Scotland, migrated over here on the Mayflower, and Manifest Destiny spread fly fishing all the way to Alaska. East Coast guys seem to be more fetishistic about their gear and will argue endlessly about arcane aspects of cane rod parabolas. Western guys tend to be less focused on their gear, and like rods that stress strength over the finish on their ferrule wraps. I, for one, enjoy light conversation about fly boxes and the relative merits of different zingers.

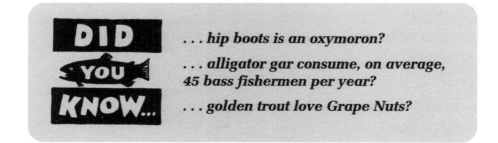

DID YOU KNOW...

. . . hip boots is an oxymoron?

. . . alligator gar consume, on average, 45 bass fishermen per year?

. . . golden trout love Grape Nuts?

Eastern Anglers	Western Anglers
Went to Harvard, majored in English Lit	Went to Boise State, three credits short
Work at Bear Stearns constantly	Shoot bears occasionally
Pay to fish	Pay to have really big satellite dish
Light Hendricksons	Light weapons fire
Those little crush caps	Real cowboy hats
Match the hatch	Chuck and duck
Size 24 Glass Beadhead Zebra Midge, 7X	Something that looks kind of like what's coming off
Grandfather taught them to fish dry	Grandfather taught them to use Helin flatfish
Orvis	Cabelas
Swisher and Richards	Swisher Sweets
Susbcribe to fly-fishing magazines	Forgot to renew subscription
South Beach diet	Slim Jims diet

recent supreme court cases involving fly fishing

As a nation of laws and not men, we are all subject to the rulings of the U.S. Supreme Court. And, of course, the purview of the court is extensive. Its jurisdiction is massive, and that includes the little-explored area of fly fishing law. We're all familiar with riparian law, but there have been a number of rulings that have touched upon the sport as we know it. The present Supreme Court has at least one known fly fisherman, but we hear he is more of a bait guy. Every area of endeavor has disputes, and the court is frequently called upon to referee. Some major fly-fishing cases include:

Local Guy v. Guy in His Hole (1980)

The court heard loud oral arguments in this case, where the plaintiff asserted that his specific fishing hole was usurped by another guy. Attorneys for the plaintiff argued that everyone from around there knew the hole in question was, in fact, the Local Guy's. The Guy in His Hole noted that the hole was not clearly marked with any sign, and he was from Denver anyway, and how the hell should he know that the hole belonged to the defendant. The court ruled in favor of the Local Guy, since the Guy in His Hole should have known better, since he was wearing a stupid hat from Patagonia.

Whetman v. U.S. Wader Companies et al. (1997)

The plaintiff argued that "shouldn't a pair of waders not leak immediately upon stepping in the water if they're new?" The court heard arguments from counsel representing the major wader manufacturers, which

noted that the implied contract with the customer did not explicitly state that their legs would stay "dry" per se. They only stated that you could wade in them, which was technically true. Of course, you can also wade in a Hickey Freeman pinstripe suit. Since lawyers were involved, the wader companies emerged victorious and continue to sell waders that leak immediately to the present day.

Bubba v. Breeding (1939)

This landmark case was a class action lawsuit that pitted bass fishermen against fly fishermen, a legal dispute that still rages. As in nuclear war, there are no winners. Numerous appeals have been filed by both parties, but each side has been locked in a death struggle. Fly fishermen note that bass fishermen wear non-natural fiber clothing and drive boats that look like they could race in the Daytona 500. Bass fishermen

observe that fly fishermen are "probably Socialists" and "may well have contributed" to National Public Radio during the pledge drive. A 2006 appeal before the court ended up with numerous injuries when the defendant's counsel referred to plaintiff's counsel as a "plastic-worm-sucking Snopes." The case may never be fully resolved.

Dry v. Wet (1802)

A case dating back to the nineteenth century and possibly having the origins of the dispute in English Common Law, Dry said that Wet's fishing style was "gauche" and "not as Sporting in the Manner of Proper Angling," and Wet asserted that Dry's fishing style was "Maddeningly frustrating with regular Frequency." The court ruled that the lead attorneys should go back to live bait until the "Great and Vexing Dispute" could be settled out of court. Appeals continue.

COMMON CASTING RULES...

THE RULES of ATTRACTION: A FLY SEEKS OUT THE ONLY POSSIBLE HANG-UP...

ZANG.

THE WIND/DROPPER FLY RULE: THE LARGER FLY FINDS THE FLESHIEST PART, AND THE SMALLER FLY HITS THE BONIEST PART...

ZANG.*

ROD SEPARATION RULE: THE FERRULES WILL LOOSEN ONLY WHEN AN AUDIENCE IS PRESENT...

ZANG*: ALL-PURPOSE FLY CASTING NOISE WORD

97

BFFFFs

Although fly fishing is reputed to be a pleasant, solitary sport, like crossword puzzles or self-abuse, eventually you wind up socializing with other people of your ilk. You'll need someone to split the gas with, someone to yell at when you can't figure out what the masking hatch is, and someone to complain bitterly about when there are six guys standing in your favorite riffle. Like any marriage, you will need to choose wisely.

I have a few, select fly-fishing friends, most of whom are north of seventy and are widely experienced in the right blood pressure medication doses. Older fly-fishing friends tend to be more philosophical about the whole thing and help to put things in perspective, like people who remember when Nixon was president. Younger fly-fishing friends tend to be all competitive about the sport and have the exact number of fish caught and strikes missed memorized. They defeat the entire purpose, which is to avoid stress. Unless they're stoned. Then they're relaxing to be around.

One of my best fly-fishing friends is ten years older and is probably my political and social diametric opposite. For some reason, this seems to work well, because we keep the conversation mostly on fly fishing and less on my personal political views, which are almost comically idealistic. I am a political cartoonist, so most things I do and believe are comical. The first requirement is that the Other Party should know when not to talk, a critical social skill sadly lacking in the 24-hour talk show era. Talking inappropriately is wrong, and conversation should be limited in most situations to how the post wing is superior to a quill wing, and in the tones reserved for a state funeral. A nice, occasional *bon mot* is good, but it has to be something about how tricky the backeddy is and not about the microscopic analysis of the 1,457 failed marriages we both have observed. No stress. It's not golf.

A typical example of a bad fly-fishing-friend conversation would be something like this:

"Yeah, I was using 7X; but the suckers keep breaking off. I should probably go to 6X. What do you think?"

"Okay. Did I tell you my prostate is enlarged?"

A more typical fly-fishing-friend conversation would go more like this:

"Yeah, I was using a size 16 CDC Gray Caddis, but then I switched to a size 18 CDC Gray Caddis and I put a little twitch on it right before it landed, you know, to kind of make it look like it was dancing, nothing happened, but then I switched back to a 14 CDC Gray Caddis and pulled a few of the fibers off the wing, you know, to make it look more sparse, and then I decided I should probably go with the bushier wing, so then I . . ."

"ZZZZZZZZZ."

"You can fool some of the trout some of the time, but you can't fool any of the trout most of the time."
—ABRAHAM LINCOLN

"Nobody ever fishes that river anymore. It's too popular." —YOGI BERRA

"We have met the enemy, and he is using bait."
—POGO

fly fishing versus golf

Every aficionado of any given sport is a passionate advocate of his or her pursuit. For example, golfers rival fly fishermen in their obsessive love of the sport. Recently, a woman golfer asserted to me, with an entirely straight face, that golf was "relaxing." Golf is a lot of things, but it is not relaxing. Drinking big martinis is relaxing; golf is horrifically stressful. That's why people get bombed in the clubhouse immediately after the eighteenth hole. Fly fishing, on the other hand, can be relaxing when the fish are hitting. And there are those who say that fly fishing is superior to every other like endeavor. Perhaps. Let's line them up, sport to sport.

Fly Fishing	Golf
No rules	Need Yale Law Degree to read rules
Little possibility of serious injury	Five iron in forehead common
Communing with nature	Communing in environmental disaster
Hooks	Hooks
Once initial gear obtained, is free	$60 a round
Bag full of gear	Bag full of gear
Solitude	Marshals
Streams and lakes	Streams and lakes are hazards
Royal Wulff	Royal pain in the ass
Go whenever the hell you want	Tee time
Lying about how many fish you caught	Lying about your score
Wet waders	Wet pants from blowing putt
Extremely heavy brush that tears your flesh	Comically groomed rough
Dog in back of pickup	Dogleg right
19th lost fly	19th hole

tips

Most fly fishermen I know act on tips faster than the Federal Bureau of Investigation. Tips are an important tool in the fly fisherman's arsenal, even if most of them turn out to be cold leads. Who among us hasn't had this conversation?

"Jeez Louise, you gotta go to (tipped location). You haven't fished there? God, it's like, AMAZING. I caught (large number) (species) in forty minutes. My rotator cuff was blown after about the eighth fish, and they were taking #10 Royal Coachmans on 4X ten feet from shore. I didn't even have to wade. It was like a hatchery."

Beware of the phrase, "It was like a hatchery." Always a bad sign.

Also beware of guides who say things like, "We got around forty yesterday, and the water temperature is the same today, and the same cfs, and my client was legally blind." This kind of preview invariably results in a day where the guide will take your $300 (and a tip) after remarking that he honestly didn't know what happened; it was unbelievable yesterday. And then he might slip in a little dig about your casting ability.

Usually tips fall somewhere in the middle. The worst kind of tip is the one that a fly-fishing magazine will give on the cover, unless it's in Canada. No one I know actually gets around to going to Canada, but if they ever do a cover story on your little stretch of the Upper Flatfooted River in your blessed home state, kiss it goodbye for two years, easy. There was this one river in Oregon I used to go to all the time. One of the local yokels who was a freelance fly-fishing writer and guide wrote about how great this part of the river was, provided the killer pattern and the name of the local fly shop, and Bada Bing!

No fish for the rest of the year. Out of state plates. Beer cans. Tangled leaders all over the place. It settled

down after a few orbits around the sun, but I still haven't bothered to go back. Thankfully, the local writer did make his rent that month for the article, so there was a happy ending.

The best tips are the ones you would get from a friend of thirty years or more. It has to be thirty years, otherwise, they might be snowing you. You just don't know. I have gotten tips from these kinds of friends with all the ceremony of the initiation rites for Skull and Bones—candles, incense, robes, the works: "You are the Anointed Recipient of the Knowledge Entrusted to the Select. Stand exactly twenty two feet from the plume at the base of the falls, your body turned at a 45 degree angle. Throw the #8 Dave's Hopper into the space between the two riffles next to the mossy rock. Hold on."

No.

I won't give you any tips.

out, damned spot!

A critical skill when speaking of fly fishing is the strict avoidance of accidentally telling someone else about your favorite spot(s). Unless they are long-time associates and maybe the executor of your estate, cageyness is king. Maintain the position that you are the President of the United States in Time of War and that you are not going to answer any questions about troop movements.

"So. You fish the (Your River Name Here)."

"Yeah. It's good."

"Where do you like to go?"

Here is where you get very, very fuzzy.

"Oh, you know. The middle part is good."

The phrase, "the middle part," is my standard response to any direct question about where I fish. Period. Unless I have known them since 1976 and they live out of state, I do not divulge any further than that. Of course, some people just don't take the hint, and being rude swine, they will press.

"What part of the middle part?"

I get fuzzier here, scowl, look down, lick my lips, run my fingers through my hair, take a sip of my coffee, sniff, sigh . . . anything.

"You know."

"You know" usually is perceived as an unsatisfactory answer, and maybe—*maybe*—I employ my verbal skills and get more specific.

"Well, you know (Name of Small Town Here)? By there." That answer can usually encompass five to ten miles of river, so I am still safe. Or not.

"What stretch?"

If they ask, "What stretch?" you're doomed. You might as well give the local tweaker your VISA number. Keep stalling. I find that feigning chest pain is a good strategy; a convincing wince and grimace has ended many an inquiry. If you're good at acting, perfect. If not, see spot ruined.

maps

I was over at the Multnomah County Library the other day, and they had an exhibition of signed first editions by Roderick Haig-Brown. If you are any sort of fly fisherman, you would know who Roderick Haig-Brown is, but if you are a newbie, he's a well-known twentieth-century (I hate typing that—makes me feel, um, almost dead) fly-fishing writer. Under the display glass was a hand-drawn map by one of Old Rod's (of course a fly fishing writer would be named Rod) buddies. It looked like an architectural blueprint.

My maps, and the maps of others, tend to be more, er, gestural. We have all gotten a map to a hotspot. Some are more detailed than others.

Invariably, maps I've gotten have either been done on some scrap of whatever worthless paper was available at the time, such as an editorial cartoon I had drawn, or, perhaps, on a piece of lined notebook paper, like this:

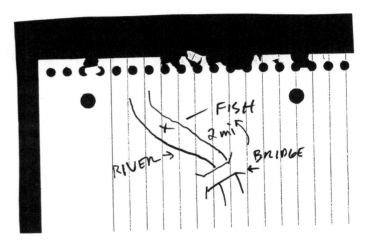

Don't ever take a map from a doctor: Or a lawyer:

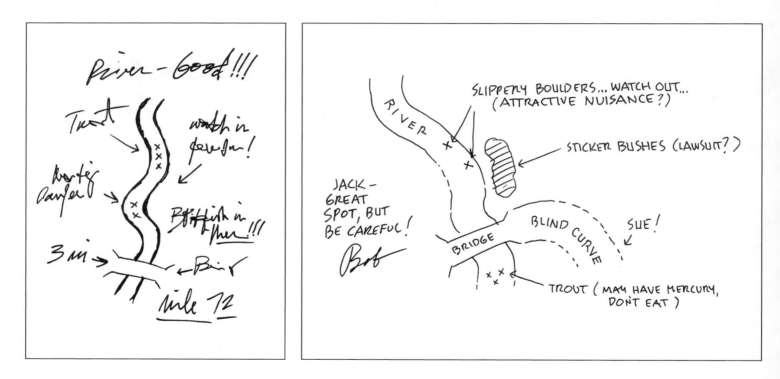

My maps tend to be kind of cartoony-looking but serviceable, if a little light on actual relevant information:

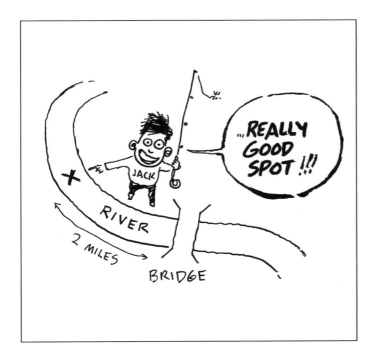

I have thoughtfully included a set of four fly-fishing maps of the United States, in case you get lost or want to take offense at the slights incurred by your particular state . . . some of our nation's states I have omitted due to space considerations, such as Alaska. Alaska is about the size of Mars. There were some states that I wasn't really sure if there was any fly fishing at all, like Mississippi (channel cats on hoppers?). You are welcome to send your contributions about your blank or misinformed state to:

The Internal Revenue Service
Ogden, Utah 84412-6906

They are always ready to help an American in trouble.

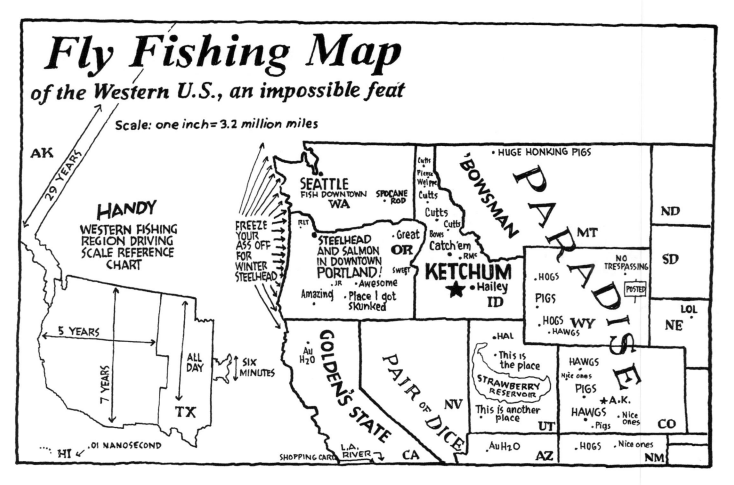

Fly Fishing Map
of the Western U.S., an impossible feat

Scale: one inch = 3.2 million miles

AK

29 YEARS

HANDY
WESTERN FISHING
REGION DRIVING
SCALE REFERENCE
CHART

5 YEARS

7 YEARS

ALL DAY

SIX MINUTES

TX

HI

.01 NANOSECOND

FREEZE YOUR ASS OFF FOR WINTER STEELHEAD

SEATTLE
FISH DOWNTOWN
WA

RLT

STEELHEAD
AND SALMON
IN DOWNTOWN
PORTLAND!
OR

SPOCANE ROD

· Great

· JR

Amazing

· Awesome

· Place I got Skunked

SWEET

Cutts
Pierce
Weippe
Cutts
Cutts
Cutts
Bows
Catch'em
RMS

'BOWSMAN

PARADISE

· HUGE HONKING PIGS

MT

ND

SD

KETCHUM
★ · Hailey
ID

· HOGS

PIGS

· HOGS **WY**
· HAWGS

NO TRESPASSING

POSTED

NE

LOL

Au H₂O

GOLDEN'S STATE

PAIR OF DICE

NV

· HAL

· This is the place

STRAWBERRY RESERVOIR

This is another place

UT

HAWGS
· Nice ones
PIGS
★ A.K.

HAWGS
· Pigs

· Nice ones

CO

SHOPPING CART

L.A. RIVER

CA

Au H₂O

AZ

· HOGS · Nice ones

NM

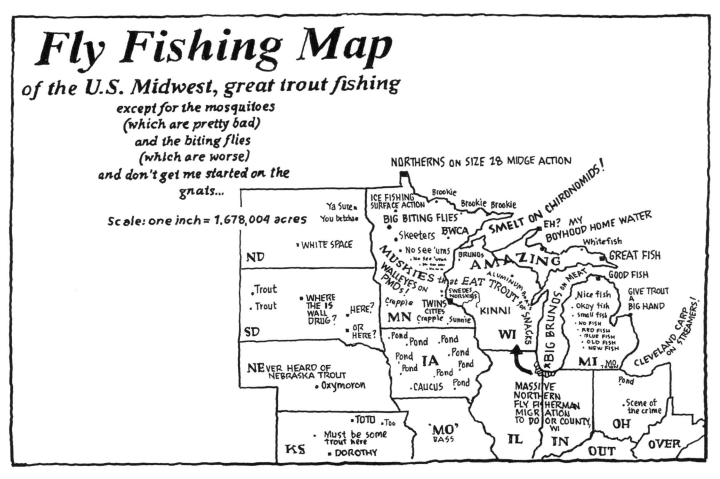

Fly Fishing Map

of the U.S. Midwest, great trout fishing

except for the mosquitoes
(which are pretty bad)
and the biting flies
(which are worse)
and don't get me started on the
gnats...

Scale: one inch = 1,678,004 acres

NORTHERNS ON SIZE 18 MIDGE ACTION

ICE FISHING SURFACE ACTION

Brookie

Brookie Brookie

SMELT ON CHIRONOMIDS!

EH? MY BOYHOOD HOME WATER

Ya Sure You betcha

BIG BITING FLIES

Skeeters   BWCA

Whitefish   GREAT FISH

• WHITE SPACE

No See 'ums

BRUNOS   AMAZING   GOOD FISH

ND

MUSKIES that EAT TROUT for SNACKS

WALLEYES ON PMDs!

ALUMINUM

SWEDES
NORSKIES

• Trout

• Trout

• WHERE THE IS WALL DRUG?

• HERE?

Crappie   TWINS CITIES

MN   Crapple   Sunnie

KINNI

WI

Nice fish
• Okay fish
• small fish
• NO FISH
• RED FISH
• BLUE FISH
• OLD FISH
• NEW FISH

GIVE TROUT A BIG HAND

SD

• OR HERE?

• Pond   • Pond   • Pond

Pond   Pond

Pond   IA

Pond   Pond   Pond

Pond   Pond

• CAUCUS   Pond

BIG BRUNOS ON MEAT

MI   MO TOWN

CLEVELAND CARP ON STREAMERS!

NEVER HEARD OF NEBRASKA TROUT

• Oxymoron

MASSIVE NORTHERN FLY FISHERMAN MIGRATION TO DOOR COUNTY, WI

Pond

• Scene of the crime

• TOTO   • Too

'MO' BASS

OH

• Must be some trout here

KS

IL   IN

OUT   OVER

• DOROTHY

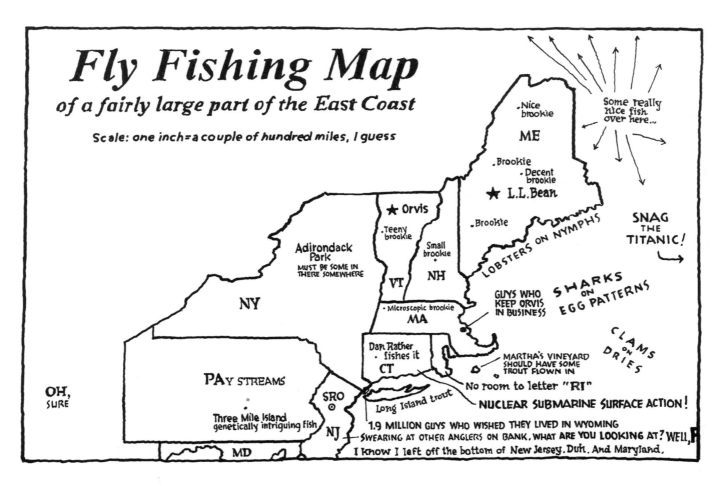

Fly Fishing Map

of a fairly large part of the East Coast

Scale: one inch = a couple of hundred miles, I guess

Some really nice fish over here...

.Nice brookie

ME

.Brookie
.Decent brookie

★ L.L.Bean

.Brookie

SNAG THE TITANIC!

★ Orvis

.Teeny brookie

Small brookie

NH

VT

Adirondack Park
MUST BE SOME IN THERE SOMEWHERE

NY

LOBSTERS ON NYMPHS

• Microscopic brookie

MA

GUYS WHO KEEP ORVIS IN BUSINESS

SHARKS ON EGG PATTERNS

CLAMS ON DRIES

Dan Rather . fishes it

CT

MARTHA'S VINEYARD SHOULD HAVE SOME TROUT FLOWN IN

No room to letter "RI"

PAY STREAMS

OH, SURE

SRO ⊙

NUCLEAR SUBMARINE SURFACE ACTION!

Long Island trout

Three Mile Island genetically intriguing fish

NJ

1.9 MILLION GUYS WHO WISHED THEY LIVED IN WYOMING
SWEARING AT OTHER ANGLERS ON BANK. WHAT ARE YOU LOOKING AT? WELL,

MD

I know I left off the bottom of New Jersey. Duh. And Maryland.

Fly Fishing Map

of the Southern United States, and bring your baseball bat to take care of the bass

Scale: one inch = oh, a fair piece

MO

MDs FLY FISH A LOT

DE

THANK YOU FOR FISHING

KY

VA

OK, LET'S GO FISHING

GORE TEX

TN

WAR AND THE TROUT GUYS

BETWEEN THE BASS GUYS

AK

Bubba

NC

SC

TROLLING OFF OF AIRCRAFT CARRIERS

WATCH OUT FOR CACTUS ON BACKCAST

JUNIOR

USE CARPET FIBERS FOR FLIES

JIMMY

THE ONLY FLY FISHERMAN IN THE ENTIRE STATE OF GEORGIA

GAR

GAR

GAR

MS

AL

GA

GAR

HUGE GAR

LA LA LA

POPPER LAKE SWAMP

GATORS ON BAETIS

GAR

TX

WHAT THEY CALL TROUT AIN'T REALLY TROUT

FL

SHARKS IN THE FILM

PLENTY OF ROOM FOR BACKCAST OFF OIL PLATFORM

BONES!

TROLL OFF CRUISE SHIP

unreliable patterns: dry flies

Pale Morning Sickness
Parachute Tangle
Comparadox
Caddissin'
Royal Pain in the Butt
Biting Mite
Biting Tarantula
Elk Hair Slurpee
Dry Humpy
Neon Adams
Ugly Stepsister
Dancing Vermin Special
Fat Ant Martha

Ratfaced Boyfriend
Al Qaeda Variant
Meet The Beetle
CDC Alert
Red Light Madame X
Main Stream Media Insects
Bed Hopper
Melanie Griffith's Gnat
Defibrillator
Little Yellow Sally Jessy
Shaquille Gordon
Political Spinner
Upwing Don King

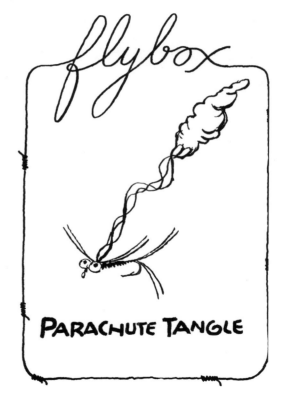

flybox

PARACHUTE TANGLE

MEET THE BEETLE   FAT ANT MARTHA   UPWING DON KING

monday evening fly fishing

"Good evening everybody, and welcome to ESPN's *Monday Evening Fly Fishing.* I'm Al Michaels, and, of course, I am joined here in the broadcast booth by John Madden. We're here on Silver Creek in stunning Sun Valley, Idaho. The conditions are perfect today for this classic match-up between the underdog fly fisherman Chuck Bates and the wily rainbows here wallowing in the grass in Silver Creek."

"Al, no question about it, you're gonna—you're gonna be seeing some GREAT fly fishing here. Bates has fished extensively on what I would call no-brainer rivers. He can throw an indicator around, and LOVES the Woolly Bugger, but when it comes right down to it, Bates doesn't really have the chops for this stream."

"John, let's go down to the action. There's Bates throwing a short line RIGHT OVER RISING TROUT. OOOOOOOOOOH! That's a BIG mistake, and that's gonna cost him."

"Look how he also is putting his own shadow on the water, Al . . . that's gonna cost him, too."

"John, Bates is now considering casting upstream to a rising 19-incher, and he is built like a VW van. He's sipping a size 20 PMD in the film, and Bates is about to make a cast."

"Al, look at that! Bates is tying on a size 4 Olive Bunny Leech! That's a HUGE mistake! He's not even TRYING to match the hatch now. He's desperately flailing a huge streamer in a dry-fly situation just to cover himself."

"DO YOU BELIEVE IN MIRACLES? Bates hooked the fish! That's just unbelievable!!!"

"You can see how that trout just accidentally got foul-hooked on the tail, and Bates is now struggling even to maintain balance let alone make any sort of headway getting that big baby in."

"John, Bates has . . . he's FALLEN IN! Let's go to the videotape on that one."

"You can see Bates tripping backwards now, and there is the splash—BOOM!!! He's down. Does he still have his rod in his hand? YES! He's up again, and the trout is still on!"

"John, Bates is now fighting against all odds to get that 19 in. AIRTIME! The fish is out of the water like Red October, and that is one big mofo. Now the fish is heading straight for Bates's legs. HE'S IN BETWEEN HIS LEGS NOW!"

"Al, that's really embarrassing. The trout's defense is KILLING Bates as he looks around for some way to salvage the situation . . . and . . ."

"THE TROUT IS OFF! THE TROUT IS OFF! That leader just snapped like a piece of spaghetti! Bates's face is a mask of dejection as he looks up to the rapidly gathering crowd of booing fans."

"John, let's not count Bates out yet. He's going to his vest now to put on a new leader and consider a new pattern. Bates still doesn't seem to realize that he's now in a spinner fall. OH, NO! Bates is rolling the heavy artillery now. Oh, my God. He's . . . he's . . ."

". . . putting on a Ford Fender."

"That is a tactical mistake and illegal on this stretch of Silver Creek. And here comes the official. Let's listen."

"AFTER A REVIEW, THE FISHERMAN WAS CAUGHT TYING ON A FORD FENDER, HAD NIGHT-CRAWLERS IN HIS POSSESSION, AND WAS CONTEMPLATING A TEXAS-RIGGED PLASTIC WORM. ILLEGAL PROCEDURE. UNSPORTSMANLIKE CONDUCT. FISHERMAN MUST GO BACK TO THE CAR AND HAVE HIS GEAR CONFISCATED."

"OHHHHHHHHH!!! OUCH!!! HE WAS EJECTED. Al, that's gonna seriously mess up his stats. That's a $700 Winston rod, a $500 Peerless reel, and about $3000 worth of flies right there. Now he's gotta go back and tell his friends. There's no free beer for Bates tonight."

"John, there's no getting around it now. Bates is out of the game. He's broke, incompetent, fishless, embarrassed, and wet."

"In short, like all fly fishermen. Now let's go back to New York for a roundup of the action of the East Coast streams."

hero shots and fish porn

Last year, while fishing in Idaho with my friend, I broke what I calculated to be my fifth camera while fly fishing. Camera A was a Canon AE-1. Dropped it in the Deschutes, but I pulled it out after two seconds: too late. My only reaction was God, I hope I they can save the pic of the brown I just caught (they did; camera ruined). Then I got a waterproof camera right before the digital thing came around. That worked great at the time, like autogyros worked great at the time. Then the New Era started. I learned just how many ways there were to crack the LCD on a digital camera (rocks, road, splash). I got another one for Christmas, and I am certain it will last well into the second week in July.

I have a number of albums full of photos—"Hero Shots"—of yours truly holding fish, and, for some odd reason, these photos are not as compelling to others as they are to me. When I have felt fatigue with houseguests, I have hauled these out at dinner parties and literally cleared the room by ten. Looking at other fishermen's photo albums is of scant interest, unless the fish in the picture is so huge that it registers an audible gasp or stunned silence. A bunch of 13-inch cutts just doesn't do it for me, unless I caught them.

"See? I was using a size 16 Blue-Winged Olive, and he just smacked it. He looked bigger when I caught him. I think." This is where even the heartiest fishing friend will only be able to muster the phrase, "That's a really nice fish," or perhaps, "Good fish," if they're tired. By the sixth "good fish," you can almost visualize their tail lights rapidly disappearing in the distance.

I was unaware of the phrase "Fish Porn" until a little while back. Some guy I know used the phrase not too long ago. I kind of recoiled. Frankly, instead of what we think of as porn, rather, it conjured up naughty calendars of the 1930s, a Vargas painting of some perky woman wearing waders and holding up a

fish with some inappropriate yet provocative caption. "Fish Porn" is just a "Hero Shot," some man holding some fish up on some river.

The camera lens has a way of rendering your fish almost invisible. I am not sure what this effect is, but it's probably like how you look in a mirror versus how you look in photos. It's got to be a huge honking trout to really fill up the frame. Furthermore, attempting to photograph your own fish is almost impossible without a third or fourth arm. You have to walk back to the bank, lay your rod down next to the fish, grab the camera, make sure the fish doesn't flop out of the picture and put him back if he does, make sure there's no shadow, take the picture, and then safely return the trout to the water. Oh, and make sure you do it in thirty seconds or less.

Next time, I will just draw the fish.

"Stand up wherever you are, go to the nearest window, and yell as loud as you can, "I'm mad as hell and I am not going to fish a backeddy ever again." —PETER FINCH

"Cinderella story. Outta nowhere. A former bait fisherman, now, about to execute a 90-foot double haul . . . it looks like a mirac . . . it's in the hole! It's in the hole! It's in the hole" —BILL MURRAY

program guide, the fly-fishing channel

5:00 A.M.—*Morning Hatch Report.*

5:30 A.M.—*Nothing's Coming Off.*

6:00 A.M.—*The 700 Dollar Rod Club.* Inspirational.

6:30 A.M.—*The Bass NASCAR Hunting Show.* Class-based ridicule show.

7:00 A.M.—*Good Morning, Clammy Waders.*

9:00 A.M.—*The Price Is Astronomical.* Game show where contestants have to guess the price of various fly-fishing equipment.

10: 00 A.M.—*Pimp My Rod.* Customizing fly-rod instructional program.

11: 00 A.M.—*Montana Fish and Game 911.* Comedy antics of game wardens.

12:00 NOON—*The Reel Life.* Paris Hilton and various other dissipated Hollywood bimbos are forced to learn how to double haul.

1:00 P.M.—*CSI: Missoula.* Crime program about people who catch and don't release.

2:00 P.M.—*Are You Smarter Than A Trout?* The never-ending question.

3:00 P.M.—*To Catch a Trout or Even a Predator, We're That Desperate.* More crime.

4:00 P.M.—*Slackline NBC.* Casting instruction.

5:00 P.M.—*Whose Line Is It, Anyway? I Think Our Leaders Are Tangled Together.*

6:00 P.M.—*Reel of Fortune!* Contestants spin large Battenkill reel for cash and prizes.

7:00 P.M.—*Yo No Se Mierda Acerca Pescando.* Spanish language fishing programming.

8:00 P.M.—*The O'Rvis Factor.* Talk/Opinion.

9:00 P.M.—*Walker, Texas Rigger.* Bass law enforcement programming.

10:00 P.M.—*Diagnosis: Muddler.* Doctors' fishing-mystery show.

11:00 P.M.—*The Schweibert Report.* Topical fly-fishing comedy.

11:30 P.M.—*Gear Eye for the Straight Guy.*

12:00 MIDNIGHT—*CFS: Stream-Flow Investigation.* Irrigators are arrested and made to disappear.

1:00 A.M.—*Hour of PowerBait.* Inspirational.

2:00 A.M.—*Desperate Housewives Who Get Boyfriends Because Their Husbands Fish All the Time.* Reality show.

3:00 A.M.—*According to Jim at The Fly Shop.* Inaccurate hotspot tips.

4:00 A.M.—*Law and Order: PMD.* Crime show about the wrong shade of mayfly.

TROUT "!" QUOTES

"Forget it, Jake . . . it's Bozeman." —JOE MANTELL

"You've got to ask yourself one question: do I feel lucky? Well, do ya, punk? Because there's no hatch." —CLINT EASTWOOD

"Those who cannot remember the cast are condemned to repeat it." —GEORGE SANTAYANA

fly-fishing upside/downside

Upside	Downside
Catching lots of fish	Slime
Box full of 2,300 flies	Can't choose one
Quiet serenity	Too much time to think about idiotic things you did from 1964 to 2008
Buying a new rod	Wondering why a rod costs as much as your car in high school
Outsmarting the fish	Think about how stupid that sounds
New water	No clue
Fresh, dry fly	It will break off in three minutes
Great cast!	Spooks 367 other fish en route
Cozy, warm waders in 45 degree water	You have to pee. Now.
The camaraderie of friends	Bunch of liars
Conversation about fly fishing	I cannot believe I'm talking about the antennae of something that lives under a rock
Sun Valley	Boise Airport
Your guide got you into a bunch of fish	$200 tip

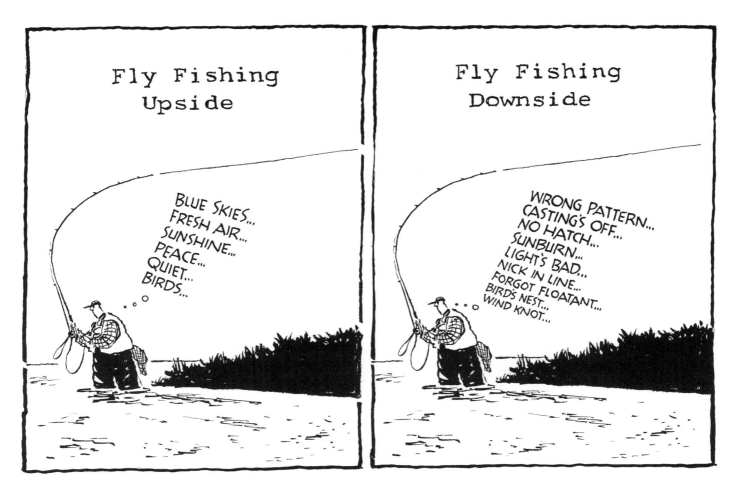

125

therapy for fly fishermen

It's a stressful, neurotic era, and we all need help from time to time, and, frankly, we're so busy with our day-to-day lives that we don't always get to the therapist the way we should. For those fly fishermen who have lost confidence, there are the following self-help books:

Chicken Feathers for the Fly-Fishing Soul

I'm Okay, Your Casting Sucks

Men Are from Mars, Fly Fishermen Are from Orvis

Healing the Inner Dragging Drift Within

Drag Co-Efficient No More

Men Who Fish Too Much

Strike Indicator Addicts and the People Who Love Them

When Bad Casts Happen to Good People

I have had more than one conversation with a fellow fly fisherman because they are actually depressed about how they did that day, or that their casting was off. Maybe they weren't hooking fish the way they used to. I too would share my own feeling of fly-fishing anxiety with close angling friends. Howell Raines, *The New York Times* editor, once wrote a great book called *Fly Fishing Through the Midlife Crisis*. I used to think of my own existence the other way: *Fly Fishing Through the Chironomidlife Crisis,* which gets right to the nub of my anxieties and takes it to the next level.

Maybe the American Psychological Association could license certified fly-fishing therapists.

"I don't know, doctor. I've lost my will to really get serious about drag-free drift. And I am deeply troubled by dark thoughts about losing big browns. I have major anxiety issues about leader material, and my hands are shaking all the time because I have to tie on 22s. And I have dreams about fishing in my underwear."

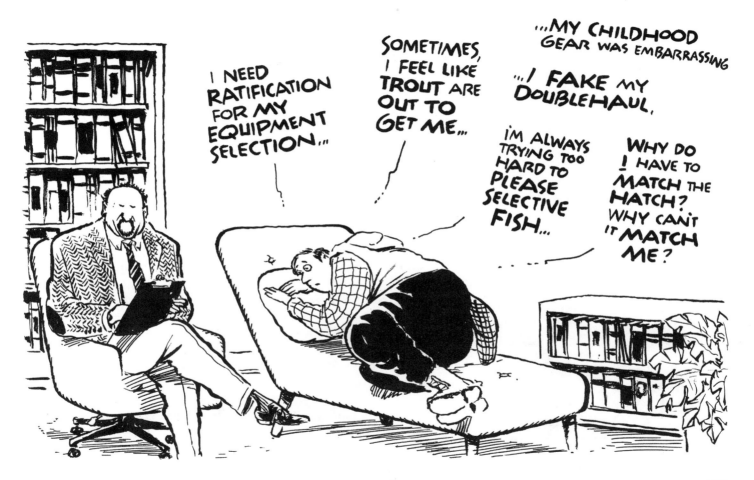

"Your mother loved you. Maybe there's a pharmaceutical solution. Take Wellbuttsection."

"I'm on Nupattern already. And Falscastin."

I suppose that therapists could theoretically go streamside, maybe open up a mobile clinic with a nice soft neoprene couch to lie down upon as you spill your guts about your unhappy fly fishing childhood. I would pay $150 an hour for that, particularly if it resulted in a few extra takes. It pencils out better than a new rod.

Most number of F-words uttered in thirty seconds after breaking off trout: 17 (Thomas N. Thomas, March 24, 1967, Tourette's Creek, Wyoming)

Number of times fly tyer messed up the wings on a #20 Adams before throwing entire fly tying kit out third story window: 12 (Howard Beale, May 8, 1988, Leeches-on-Hudson, New York)

Number of cane rods actually used by people who bought cane rods after 1970: 2

a river runs through it: judgment day

Most of us have seen the film *A River Runs Through It.* I am sure that I was not the only one who cried at the end, mostly because I was watching Brad Pitt cast. I'm sure he's a nice guy and everything, and he is married to Angelina Jolie, an angling feat of the first order. But it was a little slow at times, mostly through the scenes where his minister father, played by Tom Skerrit, was teaching him how to write. There was like a ten-minute scene of him editing, for God's sake. I think it would be cool if they made a remake of *A River Runs Through It,* but make it more of an action adventure movie. Maybe Bruce Willis plays Norman Maclean, and there are some cool explosions.

OPENING SCENE
(Young Norman is being taught
to fly cast by his father.)

FATHER: Ten and two, ten and two. Look at the metronome. Load! LOAD, NORMAN, LOAD!!! YOU NEED TO LEARN ABOUT LOADING.
NORMAN: (Takes Glock out of wicker creel.) I'm locking and loading. I'm heading to the river, and if anyone's in my spot . . . BOOOM!!!

SCENE TWO
(Norman and his brother go fishing.)

NORMAN: That's my hole, you dirtbag newspaper reporter.

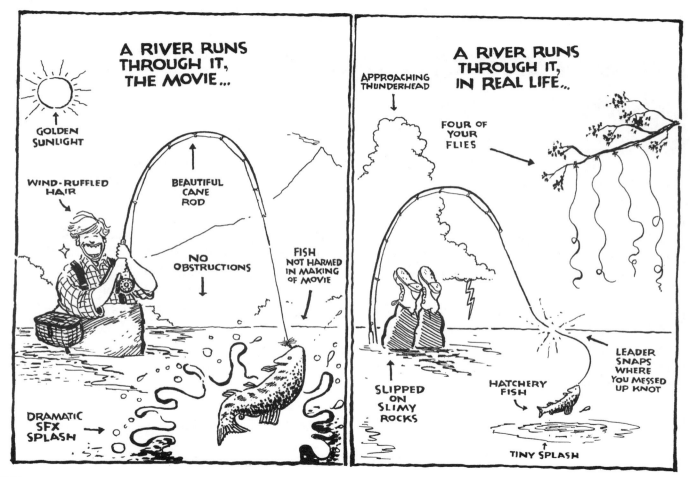

BROTHER: Shut up . . . I've been listening to your high-minded literati drivel for years. This is my hole.

NORMAN: Eat lead weights, you drunk.

(Brothers wrestle in river, Norman drags semi-conscious brother to bank, catches really nice 18-incher.)

SCENE THREE
(Norman takes hung-over brother of girlfriend fishing.)

NORMAN: Wake up, you preppy snot. And give me that damned tennis racket.

BROTHER OF GIRLFRIEND: Whuh?

NORMAN: I'll whuh you, you slick-haired mope. Take this rod.

BROTHER OF GIRLFRIEND: Do you have any worms?

NORMAN: Did you ask me if I had worms? WORMS? WE DON'T USE WORMS. (Softly, like Clint Eastwood) It's a fly-fishing movie. (Hands brother of girlfriend live grenade and throws him in river.)

SCENE FOUR
(Norman and girlfriend have long talk about future.)

GIRLFRIEND: Where are you going? You're never around.

NORMAN: I'm never around because I'm fishing. This is a fly-fishing movie, that's why I'm never around. There's a caddis hatch coming off . . . gimme the keys to the Model T, and I'll be on my way.

GIRLFRIEND: I wish I was dating a golfer. You know when they're coming home.

NORMAN: Baby, I'm sorry. But I've got a job to do. I'll be back after I limit out.

SCENE FIVE
(Norman and drunken friends steal a boat and go over a waterfall.)

NORMAN: You guys are totally faced. Let's take that boat over the waterfall.

FRIEND ONE: Great idea.

FRIEND TWO: Yeah!

FRIEND THREE: Hey, is this gonna be dangerous?

NORMAN: No. My brother's backcast is dangerous.
(Boat explodes. Friends are dazed but okay, as in
all action adventure movies after a certainly fatal
accident.)

SCENE SIX

(Sixty years later. Norman is a retired English profes-
sor. Rising sad music with violins. Shot of gnarled
hands stripping line.)

NORMAN: Dammit. The hell with this. I've got six
months to live, and I'm putting on a frog flatfish.

ROLL CREDITS.

*No trout were harmed in the making of this film. We
spray-painted some whitefish.*

"*Let your hook always be cast. In the pool where
you least expect it, will be a snag.*" —OVID

"*It depends on what your definition of 'fly' is.*"
—BILL CLINTON

"*Do not bite at the hook of pleasure unless you know
it's barbless.*" —THOMAS JEFFERSON

fly-fishing haiku

Leaders in package
So nicely wound in a coil
Explodes on contact.

———

Fly tying is zen.
You focus on the pattern.
I need new glasses.

———

Neoprene waders
So nice and warm and stretchy.
Why are my legs wet?

———

Casting is easy.
You go back to two like this.
Shit. Hooked a tree branch.

Match the hatch again,
Size 24 Adams.
Screw it. Get a worm.

———

You tie your own flies.
It's really rather simple:
Sri Lankans are best.

———

Indicators work well,
So do brass beadheads . . . deadly.
Use the dynamite.

———

Go to the fly shop,
Try to get some good intel.
Helps if you buy stuff.

fishing shops we avoid

Scuds 'R' Us
TroutMart
The Adams Family Fly Shop
Crawlers 'n' Crickets 'n' Caddis
The Impatient Angry Angler
Probably-Washed Surgical Tools
  and Fly-Tying Barn
Carp City
Fly Fishing Knotsies
VISAMAXIMA

For Tying Out Loud
The Foul Hook
Brook Trout Brothers
Bassassins
The Fly: "We're Always Open"
The Crunchy Thorax
Abercrombie and Fish
Haute Troutre
Bada Bing Fly Shop
Just Floatant

. . . mayflies taste like Wendy's Baconator?

. . . Herbert Hoover had a trout stream stocked, and that was the only thing he actually did that helped the stock market?

. . . Roger Clemens can make a cast with a 390-foot double-haul?

fly-fishing political debate

As a political cartoonist, I have to pay attention to things like presidential and congressional campaigns, in addition to whether the little windows in my Wheatley fly box open properly. I sometimes think the country would be better off if we could have a political debate strictly about fly fishing. It seems far-fetched, and yet these people get bogged down in other unsolvable political mysteries like the economy and foreign policy. At least we fly fishermen/women would have some rational basis on which to make an informed decision.

MODERATOR: Good evening and welcome to Fly-Fishing Decision. The candidates need no introduction.

GOP NOMINEE: Thank you. First, I would like to say that while we have great differences on major policy issues, the one thing we can all agree upon is the need for a rational, comprehensive national fly-fishing strategy for the twenty-first century.

DEM NOMINEE: I agree, but my opponent is actually a spin-casting meat fisherman.

GOP NOMINEE: That's simply not correct. Once again, my opponent has stooped to name-calling. I did, in fact, engage in spinning, but it was a youthful indiscretion.

DEM NOMINEE: I think the American people know when they're being spun.

GOP NOMINEE: Again, name-calling doesn't move the debate forward. The fact is, I think the real divide here is between dry and wet.

DEM NOMINEE: More demagoguery. My opponent says he's a populist wet-fly fisherman, but the fact is that he's an elitist dry-fly fisherman.

GOP NOMINEE: Fine. I have done both.

DEM NOMINEE: Flip-flopper.

GOP NOMINEE: Does using a dropper count?

DEM NOMINEE: This just shows my opponent can't make the right call for the American people. He's wishy-washy. He wants it both ways: wet and dry.

GOP NOMINEE: My opponent is only interested in dividing us. My opponent once again resorts to the politics of personal destruction. The fact is, we have a photograph of my opponent using Power-Bait in 1972. I hope the American people see these attacks for what they are: a PowerBait grab.

MODERATOR: Time's up. Next week, the candidates debate bait.

Number of impulse murders committed by fly fishermen attempting to fish on Opening Day in New Jersey: 19 (April 20, 2005)

Heaviest combined weight of a limit of six brook trout taken: 14 ounces (August 19, 1990)

Largest carp ever accidentally taken while fly fishing: 369 pounds, 2 ounces

Number of "Yes, sirs!" cheerfully and chirpily uttered in two-minute period while chatting with fish-and-game officer when an angler left his license in his other vest: 34

fly fishing with shakespeare
(william, not the tackle company)

"Beware the Browns of March." —*Julius Caesar*

"What spools these Hardys be?" —*A Midsummer Night's Dream*

"Good night, sweet bead head Prince." —*Hamlet*

"Friends, Romans, countrymen, lend me your Hare's Ears." —*Julius Caesar*

"Uneasy lies the head that wears a size 6 Woolly Bugger." —*King Henry IV, Part 2*

"The gods are just, and of our pleasant vices make instruments to plague us, like whip-finishers." —*King Lear*

"Is this a fly rod I see before me, the handle toward my hand? Come, let me clutch thee." —*Macbeth*

"By the pricking of my thumbs, something wicked this way comes. I forgot to clip the barb." —*Macbeth*

"Et tu, Brule?" —*Julius Caesar*

"A very ancient and fishlike smell. I really should get rid of this vest." —*The Tempest*

"Some men are born bait, some men achieve baitness, and some have baitness thrust upon them." —*Twelfth Night*

"Blow, blow thou winter wind,
Thou art not so unkind
As a wind knot." —Sonnet

"I pray thee cease thy counsel,
Which falls into mine ears as profitless
As water in a sieve. I don't need your goddamn'd
Advice on my backcast." — Sonnet

"Though I am not naturally honest,
I am so sometimes by chance. I swear
I caught thirty-eight in two hours." — Sonnet

trout advertising slogans

I am constantly reminded—by people who basically irritate me—that everything's about branding. You've got to agree, in a way. I wonder what life was like before advertising? Was it less stressful, or did you have to wander aimlessly in 1622 looking for the best blacksmith or horseshoe repair joint? I suppose it must have been on Manhattan Island, after the first marketing guy screwed the resident Native Americans for twenty-four bucks, that they then turned to the rest of the population. I have been reading about fly fishing in magazines for years, and I cannot, at this moment, come up with a memorable fly-fishing advertising slogan. I found these in a drawer.

"I have good news . . . I just saved a bunch of money on my car insurance by switching to nymphs."

"Caddis Pupa: It's what's for dinner."

"Pale Morning Duns, the other other white meat."

"The incredible, edible egg pattern."

"For all you do, this bug's for you."

"See what browns can do for you."

"The few, the proud, the marine life."

"Got milt?"

Any major fly-fishing advertisers are free to contact me at www.iwilltakeyourmoneyhappily.com.

unreliable patterns: wet flies

Rusty Scud
Burrowing Tick Emerger
San Juan Tapeworm
Tie Down Kangaroo
Itchy Flea
Dave's Cockroach
Muddler Miniature Poodle
Woolly Housefly
Leadwing Bratwurst
Cialis Minnow
Husky Bottomfeeder
Grizzly Predator
Grey Root Special

Cream Curdler
Squirmin' Divorcee Nymph
Screaming Harpie
Flying Nunchuk
Larry King Larva
Special Prosecutor
Sharon Stonefly
Victoria's Secret
Bipolar Bear Streamer
Brother-in-law Leech
Segmented Personality
Rubber Leg Drunk

flybox

LARRY CRAIG'S
FLY
FOR TROLLING

LARRY KING LARVA

WHITEWATER WET
WITH TRAILING
NYMPH

FLY FORMERLY KNOWN
AS BEAD-HEAD
PRINCE

fly fishing versus everything else: what's better?

Fly Fishing	Football	Determination
Serene life	Threating injuries	Fly fishing

Fly Fishing	Baseball	Determination
Strikes	Strikes at 95 mph	Fly fishing

Fly Fishing	Soccer	Determination
Butt sections	Headbutts	Fly fishing

Fly Fishing	NASCAR	Determination
Roaring rapids	Roaring, rapid cars	Fly fishing

Fly Fishing	Politics	Determination
Flopping fish, bites, action	Flip-flops, sound bites, inaction	Fly fishing

Fly Fishing	Yardwork	Determination
Weeds in water	Weeding, watering	Fly fishing
Fly Fishing	Martha Stewart	Determination
Quality time	Jail time	Duh
Fly Fishing	American Idol	Determination
Salmon	Simon	Fly fishing
Fly Fishing	Britney Spears	Determination
Relaxing	Rehabbing	Fly fishing
Fly Fishing	Dating	Determination
Expensive pain in the ass	Expensive pain in the ass	Tie

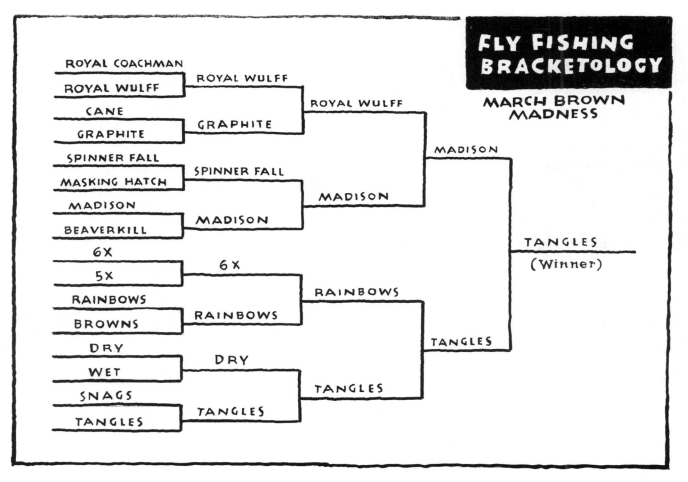

more fly-fishing haiku

Spend three bills on guide,
He'll put you in the good spots.
Get skunked is the rule.

———

It's a spinner fall!
Quick! Tie on a size twenty!
Where is the hook eye?

———

Tell wife you're fishing,
You will be back in three weeks.
Then meet her lawyer.

———

I need a new rod
You know, I certainly do.
I own two hundred.

Hmm. Cane or graphite?
It is an age-old question.
You will break the cane.

———

How many you catch?
"Oh, I got thirty or so."
The goddamn liar.

———

Windy again,
Could not make a decent cast.
Gonna start bowling.

the amazing similarities between fly fishing, lincoln, and kennedy

The words fishing, Lincoln, and Kennedy each have seven letters.

Fly fishing is performed on water. Kennedy and Lincoln both drank water.

Kennedy and Lincoln were both leaders. Fly fishing has leaders.

Kennedy often had his fly down. Some flies are fished down. Lincoln had a down personality.

You will often see Lincoln Navigators parked by rivers.

Fly fishing involves trout, and trout was often served to both Lincoln and Kennedy.

The Potomac is right by the White House, where Kennedy and Lincoln both lived. There are rivers that flow into the Potomac where you can fly fish.

Kennedy and Lincoln both had millions of dollars in their budgets for equipment. Fly fishermen have millions of dollars in their budgets for equipment.

Kennedy and Lincoln both had brothers named Orvis.

Kennedy and Lincoln both were president during stressful times of great crisis. Fly fishing is often a stressful time of great crisis.

Kennedy and Lincoln both were succeeded by men named Johnson. There is a spinning reel company named Johnson, which you could use with a bubble and fly.

Fly fishing can be done in both Massachusetts and Illinois, the home states of Kennedy and Lincoln.

Kennedy, Lincoln, and fly fishermen all experienced significant backlash.

blogs and websites

Now that we are in the Age of the Internets (George W. Bush), we are confronted with a selection of fly-fishing blogs. Some of them are pretty straightforward, like travelogues, and others are more technical and how-to. Mostly, they have the usual hero shots and exclamations about how hard the 22-inch brown smashed my Gray Ghost. All this is fine. I know I should be blogging about fly fishing, but whatever free time I have (practically none) for now is consumed by actually attempting to fish and writing humorous japes for this book.

I actually do have a fly-fishing blog (www.jackohman.com—clever, huh?), but I haven't really gotten around to putting much of anything on it yet. I will, I swear. Blogging usually consists of microscopic information conveyed to a microscopic audience, but I would really like to see some more . . . er . . . barbed commentary.

Here is a selection of my favorite sites:

        www.orvishasmylifesavings.com
        www.whyarerodssixbills.com
        www.guidesIwanttoslug.com/hitmen
        www.explainthewhipfinishonemoretime.com/good-luck
        www.drivefourhourstoseeonerise.com
        www.putyourrodinthewatersonooneseesyouhaveafishon.com
        www.threebucksforaflywhatthehell.com/sri-lanka-economy-total-GNP
        www.getoutofmyriffleyounewyorkSOB.com/interlopers
        www.noIamnotgoingtogiveyoumylastwoollybugger.com/chronic-moochers
        www.godIwishIhadarapalanow.com/cheating

www.ijustspentseventybucksforchickenfeathers.com/mark-up

www.ifIhavetotieanotherdropperonIamgoingtoscream.com

www.boxfullofrustyflies/there-goes-five-hundred-bucks/squandered

www.ifIstickonalittlePowerBaitwho'sgonnaknow.com/moral-quandary

www.whyissomeonealwaysinmyspot.com/philosophical-question

www.hatcheryfishwhyeffingbother.com/meat-fishermen

www.brooktroutthesizeofyourthumb.org/fish-NewEngland

www.trynottolooklikeayuppiewhengoingintoIdahobar.com/no-eye-contact/lose-the-patagonia

www.Ineedamastersinentomologytomatchthishatch/rapidly-becoming-work

www.Ileftmynon-residentlicenseinthetruckIsweartoGod/likely-story/big-fine/slicker

www.stopcallingitapoleit'sarodgoddamnit.com/get-it-straight/stop-embarrassing-yourself

www.explainwhyapieceofplasticstringisfortyclams.com/no-good-reason

www.chroniclyingaboutfishsizeandlength.com/sexual-issues

www.racingformulaonecarsischeaperthanflyfishing.com/home-equity-line-of-credit-tapped-out

DID YOU KNOW...

. . . scientists have discovered trout actually have a verbal two word vocabulary consisting of "refusal" and "spooked?"

. . . Canada has over 8 million illegal immigrants, all of them Americans looking for new water?

. . . the NSA has a black budget for "fly shop intel?"

matchthehatch.com: fly-fishing personals

Mustn't Love Drag

SWM, 39, 6'0", 175, obsessed with presentation, to engage in mutual casting lessons, naughty backcasts, and bawdy badinage about scuds. No cross-dressers. Not into that kind of drag.

I Hate Backeddies

SWF, 32, 5'5", 135, can't throw into backeddy to save my life. Help! Will you show me how to do it? Any other physics-defying social skills welcome!

Big Western River Double-Haul Guy Seeks SWF For Astronomically Long Casts

SWM, 38, 6'2", 205, can make an 80-foot throw land on that little twig, twitch it, drop it off, and hook 20-incher on a size 22. I also lie about a lot of other stuff.

No Worms Allowed

Tired of the baiting game, SWF, 34, 5'7", 128, needs to find true fly-fishing love after being involved with basshole. Want to get out of frightening Ranger boat preferred by Iranian Navy and learn the subtle art of tying on something that doesn't get slime all over my hands. No worms, leeches, shrimps. Waiting with baited breath.

Old School Cane Seeks Same in SWF

SWM, 79, 5'8", 138, refuses to try out graphite. This old bamboo rod still works fine, just needs time to haul. May talk fiberglass if that's your bag, but no other composite materials. Call me on rotary dial phone and we'll drive to fishing hole in 1956 International Harvester.

Kinks in My Leader

SWM, 40, 5'11", 200, has serious kinks to work out in leader. Will try anything once! I'm in knots! Friends describe me as seriously tangled. I look good in the package, but the second I get out, well . . . I am a mess!

Psychodrama over Nothing

Angry GWM, 44, 5'10", 160. Seriously OCD about the smallest points of fly fishing. Want to get into a shouting match over ferrules? I'm your guy. Need to scream at someone about parachute hackle versus conventional hackle? I can do that. In fact, I can get apoplectic over virtually anything regarding any point of contention in fly fishing . . . what did you just say and what did you mean by that?

My Wife Doesn't Understand My Fly Fishing

SWM, 50, 5'11", 210, seeks SWF for discreet fishing affair. No sex, just sit and read a book and act like you're not bored out of your mind and watch me while I fish. It's not asking a lot. In turn, I will feign interest in your stupid book club and your monologue about why olive oil is better than butter.

Line-Weight Issues

SWF, 43, 5'6", 190, a little heavy on the old shooting head, if you get my drift. Squeezing a 6 weight into a reel designed for a four weight. Tried everything, but I am still weight forward and my butt section could use some work, too. Great sense of humor!

Catch and Release?

SWM, 45, 6'0", 180, looking for a fly fisherwoman with benefits for one-stream stand. We meet at the river, fish all day with reckless abandon, and then go our separate ways. No lines attached.

group fishing

Although fly fishing is billed as a solitary pursuit, akin to being a sniper or, even more odious, a cartoonist, it's actually more often than not a group enterprise. For example, I often go with at least one other person to make sure that I drown safely. Sometimes, I will go with a group of three other guys and, a few times a year, with maybe eight or ten.

When I get up into Eight-Fellow-Fisherman Land, I get nervous. Not that they're not all fine people and good friends, but I just get . . . weird. It doesn't seem right to have eight other people going on a fishing trip, unless you're working on an Alaska fishing boat. We usually camp up in Idaho (somewhere) in the early fall. Sometimes, we rent a cabin, but usually we're in this camp that at times resembles Camp Lejuene. We line up for food. We do KP. We get water. We do close marching drills. Stuff like that.

Of course, evenings are fun. We have animated political conversations, talk about philosophy, play word games, or make observations about each other's flatulence (sorry, it's a bunch of guys). Many people in the party also drink alcoholic beverages. Hard to believe, but no one really gets too unruly, except during election years. No, all this stuff is fun. The trouble is deciding who gets to fish where.

Even on a stretch of water that probably has 30 fishable miles, there are small, quiet conversations that take place out of earshot of the Others. Two or three guys will slip off to the side of the group after dinner, and you know damned well that they're not talking about alternative fuels. No, they are conspiring. They're conspiring to get to your water.

I don't want to name names here. I won't. One of the members of our group is famous for making up names for the various stretches of water we fish. We also keep an elaborate bound log that each member of the group gets most years. One of the stretches of river is called, cleverly enough, Jack's Slot. It's called the

Jack's Slot because I, enterprising wader that I am, discovered this nothing-looking little slot WAY across a nothing-looking flat. The first year I went over there, I just . . . um . . . caught a lot of fish. The mistake was reporting back that I had done so. You really have to work to get to Jack's Slot, believe me. For years, I have caught tons of fish out of Jack's Slot. I would usually go over to it with one—one—of the other guys. As it was Jack's Slot, I hosted. You know what I'm talking about if you fish at all. You have your own spots, and if someone else goes into that spot, well, you get upset.

One day, I came back to camp and one of our party reported cheerfully and chirpily that he had fished Jack's Slot, and really hammered them.

God, was I mad.

Of course, stoic Minnesota Norwegian that I am, I said nothing. I just listened to this . . . this interloper . . . go on and on about how well he did in Jack's Slot. Finally, I couldn't take it anymore. I said, "Hey (unnamed friend), did you just hear yourself? You just talked about how well you did in Jack's Slot. That's JACK'S Slot, not (unnamed friend)'s Slot." I mean, it's like stealing a friend's VISA number and then bragging about how much money you saved at Nordstrom and Morton's Steakhouse.

Silence. Busted.

He'll never do that again.

Of course, I wasn't mean about it. I just brought it up. Just sayin'.

Then I remembered I had just fished in the hole named after him earlier in the day.

Once the water is divvied up after conspiracy conversations, off we go in our respective inefficient vehicles. We drive to our well-planned conspiracy hole, fish for awhile (it usually doesn't pan out), then one of us will turn to the other and say, "We should go to the Rabid Marmot Water," or whatever it is, and we go to the Rabid Marmot Water, and there're three guys from your camp happily flailing away.

Then we have to go to Plan C: prospecting. If I have five or more days on a trip (I usually don't), then I do like to prospect a bit. You know, while away an afternoon up some little creek, and you don't really care that much whether you get anything or not. Doesn't matter. But if I have driven 565 miles, most of it uphill, I usually like to know that there will be large, semieasy-to-catch, fat—preferably stupid—trout. Oh, and on dries, please. Thank you.

All that said, I do prefer going with maybe three other people. Breaks up the conversational dynamics and you can split off into two groups. There is plenty of water for all, and it works out fine. No fancy camp kitchens to set up. If you go with one other person, you better make sure that you can have an eight-hour conversation in the car. That can be hard to do. I usually like to go with my Conservative Friend, so we can yell at each other most of the time when we're not talking about fishing. If you go with someone you agree with, it gets boring, fast. Alternatively, you should go with someone you have known for twenty years or so, in order to replay The Greatest Hits of Your Previous Trips: "Hey—remember that one riffle we fished?"

"Yeah."

And, without any real reference point for your friend other than that, you can spend a half hour describing the time you switched from 5X to 6X in that riffle, and, by God, that did the trick: Tinkers to Evers to Chance. QED. He can then counter-regale you with some turgid, massively footnoted anecdote about the time, in that same riffle, that he was using a #14 Caddis Pupa, but then he went to a #16 Comparadun, and he caught twelve in thirty minutes. You nod, knowing that he can fill the airtime too. Then it's your turn to bore the hell out of him for twenty minutes.

. . . there are no trout in Bismarck, North Dakota?

. . . the Royal Coachman has never actually caught any fish?

. . . NASA developed a fly tying machine in 1967, but has kept it in a secret bunker at Area 51?